MW01200225

HOW TO WRITE A NOVEL USING THE
SNOWFLAKE METHOD

RANDY INGERMANSON

Ingermanson Communications, Inc.

CONTENTS

Chapter One

THE IMPRACTICAL DREAM

G oldilocks had always wanted to write a novel.

She learned to read before she went to kindergarten.

In grade school, she always had her nose in a book.

In junior high, the other kids thought she was weird, because she actually *liked* reading those dusty old novels in literature class.

All through high school, Goldilocks dreamed of writing a book of her own someday.

But when she went to college, her parents persuaded her to study something *practical*.

Goldilocks hated *practical*, and secretly she kept reading novels. But she was a very obedient girl, so she did what her parents told her. She got a very practical degree in marketing.

After college, she got a job that bored her to tears—but at least it was practical.

Then she got married, and within a few years, she had two children, a girl and then a boy. She quit her job to devote full time to them.

As the children grew, Goldilocks took great joy in introducing them to the stories she had loved as a child.

When her son went off to kindergarten, Goldilocks thought

about looking for a job. But her resume now had a seven-year hole in it, and her practical skills were long out of date.

The only jobs Goldilocks could qualify for were minimum wage.

She suddenly realized that being practical had made her horribly unhappy.

On a whim, Goldilocks decided to do the one thing she had always wanted more than anything else—she was finally going to write a novel.

She didn't care if it was *impractical*.

She didn't care if nobody would ever read her novel.

She was going to do it just because she wanted to.

For the first time in years, she was going to do something *just for herself*.

And nobody was going to stop her.

On a beautiful morning in September, after sending her children off to school, Goldilocks sat down at her computer and opened a new document. She wanted to write an exciting story packed with romance and suspense. It would star a handsome man and a beautiful woman and an evil villain during a dangerous time—the last year of the Third Reich.

She typed the first word of her novel: "The."

Goldilocks stopped typing. She stared at the screen. She had a million different choices for the next word. And a million for the word after that.

The possibilities were endless.

And she couldn't type the next word. There were too many possibilities.

She didn't dare make a mistake. If she got started in the wrong direction, then she'd have to backtrack, and that would be horrible.

She'd waited so *long* to write this story. It had to be perfect. It had to be her own, special story. She could not afford to get it wrong.

Goldilocks stared at the screen for a full hour. Stared at that one horrible, miserable, stupid word. "The."

She knew she could write. Knew she had talent. Knew she had a story bubbling up inside her. But she couldn't seem to get it onto the page.

Finally she closed the document and cried.

For about five minutes.

Then she dried her eyes and took a deep breath. She wanted so desperately to write a novel. She was not going to let her lack of knowledge stop her.

All she needed was someone to guide her. A mentor. Somebody to point the way.

Goldilocks opened her web browser and went looking for a class or a workshop or a lecture on how to write a novel.

Surely, there was somebody who could teach her how to achieve her dream.

She quickly discovered a writing conference right in her own town that would be starting *tomorrow*.

Goldilocks was so excited, she could hardly breathe. She signed up for the conference online. Tomorrow, she was going to learn the secret of writing a novel.

The next day, Goldilocks arrived at the conference center just on time. She parked right outside the coffee shop and ran inside the main building and picked up her registration packet. She had already read the schedule and had found exactly the workshop she needed. "Outlining Made Easy—How to Plot Your Novel."

Goldilocks raced to the room where the workshop was being given.

Nearly a hundred students were packed into the classroom.

She found a seat near the back.

The teacher was a large male bear who introduced himself as Papa Bear. "I've been teaching for forty years, and many of my students have gotten published. The secret to writing a novel is to plot it out in advance. My best student was Robert Ludlum, and he did pretty well for himself."

Goldilocks began taking notes.

She learned that an outline for a novel wasn't like the outlines she had learned to make in third grade, using roman numerals and capital letters and lots of indenting.

She learned that when novelists talk about an *outline*, they mean a *synopsis*—a summary of the story, telling the highlights of the plot.

She learned that serious outliners often make five or ten synopses, polishing and polishing until the final version is perfect.

She learned that a synopsis can be fifty to a hundred pages long. Or more.

Goldilocks skipped the next workshop and went to the coffee shop right next to the conference center. She bought herself a latte and sat outside at a shaded table in the secluded back patio and began writing her synopsis. She typed furiously for three pages and then stopped to read what she'd written.

She couldn't believe how awful it seemed. Her story was *boring*.

But she refused to give up. She had three pages down, ninety-seven to go.

Goldilocks kept typing, straight through until lunchtime. When she checked her progress, she had written eleven pages.

And she hated her story.

She never wanted to think about it again.

Goldilocks felt horrible. She knew that outlining worked for some writers. Robert Ludlum was a great writer, and she had enjoyed many of his novels.

But outlining didn't work for her.

She refused to believe she was stupid.

She knew she had talent as a writer.

She knew she had a story inside her.

But outlining the way Papa Bear taught was too boring for her.

During lunch, Goldilocks leafed through the program and saw another workshop that looked better. "Writing Your Novel Organically—How to Unlock the Inner You."

Goldilocks ran to the workshop and got there a few minutes early.

The teacher was a large female bear with soft, warm, chocolate-brown eyes who introduced herself as Mama Bear. She smiled at Goldilocks and asked her name and what she was writing. By the time the workshop was ready to begin, Goldilocks knew she'd found a friend.

Mama Bear explained that the secret to writing a novel was to simply let it well up out of your soul. No need to plot your novel in advance. That was for boring, accountant-type writers—the kind who had to have a six-step procedure for kissing their wives.

The class laughed at that.

Goldilocks felt herself relaxing. Yes, this was what she'd been wanting. Organic writing sounded like a very natural way to write.

Mama Bear spent the full hour talking about the benefits of writing organically, or as some writers called it, "writing by the seat of your pants."

"I've had many students over the years," Mama Bear said. "Stephen King writes this way. There's nothing to it. You just sit down and watch the story unfold in your mind, and then you write it down."

Goldilocks could hardly wait to get out of the workshop so she could start writing organically.

The instant the workshop ended, Goldilocks raced back to the coffee shop and opened a fresh new document on her computer and began typing furiously. The story welled up out of her soul.

For three whole letters.

"The."

Goldilocks waited expectantly. Closed her eyes and waited for more words to well up out of her soul.

Waited.

Waited.

But nothing more came.

Goldilocks slammed the lid of her laptop shut and began pacing back and forth.

Was there something wrong with her?

She didn't think so.

She knew what she wanted to write about—sort of.

She knew it was a good story—probably.

But the storyline wasn't clear in her mind, and she was terrified to just start rambling.

She felt like she needed to know where the story was going before she started.

Mama Bear's organic method of writing seemed too squishy and vague for her.

❄

*G*oldilocks grabbed her conference schedule and scanned it desperately.

The title of one of the major tracks leaped out at her: "How to Write a Novel When You Hate Outlining and Hate Organic Writing."

That sounded like it had been created exactly for Goldilocks.

She stuffed everything in her backpack and hurried toward the classroom.

She reached it just in time and stopped in the doorway, looking for a seat.

There was only one place left—in the very front row.

Everybody was looking at Goldilocks as she scurried in.

Her ears burning, Goldilocks hurried to the chair and slouched low into it.

One thing was for sure.

She was going to keep trying until she found a method of writing that worked for her.

She would never give up her dream of writing a novel.

Never, ever, ever.

Chapter Two

YOUR TARGET AUDIENCE

The teacher was a tiny, energetic bear who introduced himself as Baby Bear.

Goldilocks thought he couldn't be much more than three feet tall, and she wondered why the conference organizers would hire such a young and inexperienced teacher.

"How many of you have tried outlining your novel and hated it?" Baby Bear asked.

Several students raised their hands, including Goldilocks.

"And how many of you have tried 'organic writing' and couldn't make it work?" Baby Bear asked.

A different set of students raised their hands.

Goldilocks wondered if she was the only person who had tried both methods.

"This workshop is the first in a series—a major track that will continue for the rest of the conference," Baby Bear said. "I'll teach you a method that tens of thousands of writers around the world are using right now to write their novels. It might work for you, and then again it might not. Different writers are different, and your first mission as a novelist is to find the method that works best for you."

Goldilocks sat up in her chair. She liked the fact that Baby Bear wasn't making any wild promises.

"I need a volunteer to help me teach this first session," Baby Bear said. "Who wants to help? I need somebody who's thought quite a bit about their story and wants to start writing, but just can't seem to get started."

An old woman sitting next to Goldilocks raised her hand. "I've got a story about an old woman who went to the cupboard and it was bare."

Baby Bear squinted at the old woman's name tag. "Ah, Mrs. … Hubbard. Are you writing women's fiction, then?"

Mrs. Hubbard shook her head. "No, I don't think so. I don't know what women's fiction is. The story is mostly about the cupboard. It was bare, you see. That's all I know about the story, so far."

"I'm terribly sorry, ma'am, but I'm looking for a volunteer who's a bit further along than that," Baby Bear said. He pointed to a very large pig sitting in the second row. "What sort of novel are you writing, sir?"

The pig stood up and straightened his black bow tie. "Actually, I'm not writing the story myself. I'm looking for a coauthor to help me write a story about a young, industrious pig who rises from poverty to become a powerful and wealthy captain of industry." He polished his spectacles on his tie. "It's a bit autobiographical, but I'm no writer myself, and I just need somebody to help me put the words down. This book should write itself."

Baby Bear read the pig's name tag. "Well, Mr. Little Pig, you may just find yourself a coauthor here at this conference, but I'm looking for a volunteer who's actually a *writer*. Somebody who's already started writing and got stuck."

Goldilocks felt her cheeks burning. She covered her face with her hands.

Baby Bear pointed at her. "Are you raising your hand, young lady?"

Goldilocks felt frozen with fright. She couldn't possibly talk about her story in front of all these smart and savvy writers. That would be just too humiliating.

Baby Bear padded over to stand in front of her and took her hands in his warm, furry paws. "What kind of novel are you writing?"

"I'm … not quite sure what to call my kind of story," Goldilocks said. "There's a handsome man in it. And a beautiful woman. And an evil villain. And it's set during World War II. And the story is going to be very exciting."

Baby Bear nodded and tugged on her hand. "Very good, we can work with that. Come up to the hot seat and tell me about it."

"But … all these people," Goldilocks said. "They're staring at me."

Baby Bear led her up to a chair beside the front table and sat her down and then jumped up to sit on the table with his short legs hanging over the edge. "Pretend there's nobody here but you and me. Tell me more about your story. Is it a romance novel?"

"Not … quite," Goldilocks said. "They do fall in love, but it's not only romance. The story is set right before D-Day, and there's a lot going on. There are commandos on an important mission, and …" She sighed. "I don't know how to explain it."

"You're doing fine," Baby Bear said. "Is it a suspense novel?"

"I'm not exactly sure what that is."

"A suspense novel is mainly about the plot. Something awful is about to happen, and the hero is there to prevent it. Or something wonderful is about to happen, and the hero is there to make it happen."

"Well … that's close, but not quite," Goldilocks said. "My heroine is a French woman living in a small village during the German occupation. And my hero is an American agent who parachutes in behind enemy lines on an important mission, but he breaks his leg."

"And these two meet up?" Baby Bear asked.

"Yes, in chapter 1. And she takes care of him and he tells her about his mission and she wants to help him but he's falling in love with her and he's afraid that the Nazis might kill her, but then she argues with him that just having him in her house has already put her in danger, and she's a widow with a young daughter and—"

"Whoa, whoa, whoa!" Baby Bear held up a furry paw. "You've got a fantastic story there! How much of it is written already?"

Goldilocks felt her face turning hot again. "Not … very much."

"Well, I love it!" Baby Bear turned to the class. "How many of you like her story?"

Everybody raised their hands. Mrs. Hubbard was sitting forward in her chair and staring at Goldilocks as if she were somebody famous. Little Pig was leaning back in his chair, studying her with an appraising eye.

Baby Bear jumped off the table and peered at her name tag. "I suppose we should back up and make some introductions. Your name is … Goldilocks." He studied her face intently. "You look familiar. Have you ever been to one of my writing classes before?"

Goldilocks shook her head. The only time she had ever seen a bear who looked anything like Baby Bear was a long time ago, on a perfectly dreadful day that she wanted very much to forget. "I'm just starting out learning how to write."

"Well, you obviously have talent."

"I do?" Goldilocks said.

"Of course!" Baby Bear said. "The main purpose of fiction is to give your reader what I call a 'powerful emotional experience.' And your book sounds like it's going to generate all sorts of powerful emotions."

Goldilocks felt her heart going pitty-pat. "When I was younger, everybody criticized me for being 'too emotional.'"

Baby Bear gave her a long, searching look. "Why would you care what other people think about you?"

"Because it matters!" Goldilocks said.

"Why does it matter?"

Goldilocks just shook her head in exasperation. "Because it does!" Everyone must think she was very foolish to be arguing with a bear.

Baby Bear simply shrugged. "For a novelist, being 'too emotional' is often a good thing. The only thing you have to sell is your emotional experiences."

Heads were nodding all around the room.

Goldilocks felt a warm feeling welling up inside of her. The other writers seemed to like her. They understood her. She hoped none of them noticed that she hadn't done a good job on her hair this morning.

Baby Bear began pacing. "So, Goldilocks, you're writing a romantic suspense novel set in World War II. That's what we call your category."

"Why is that important?" Goldilocks asked.

Baby Bear grinned. "When the bookstore gets copies of your book from your publisher, they need to know which shelf to put them on. As soon as they know your category, they've got their answer."

Goldilocks had never thought about that.

"Now I want you to imagine that you've published your novel and it's on the appropriate shelf at your local bookstore. Six people walk into the store. An older man and woman. A younger man and woman. A boy and a girl. Can you see them?"

Goldilocks nodded.

"Which one of them is going to be interested in your book?" Baby Bear asked.

"Well … all of them, I suppose," Goldilocks said. "I want my novel to be a best seller. I want everybody to buy it."

Baby Bear just looked at her. "Let me tell you a bit more about these people. The older man is wearing a fishing cap. The older woman has on gardening gloves. The younger man is dressed like an accountant. The younger woman has two children clutching her hands, a boy and a girl. Which of those six people is going to be most interested in your book?"

"The younger woman," Goldilocks said. "The other adults all came looking for nonfiction books, but that younger woman definitely wants my novel. And it's too grown-up for the children."

Baby Bear rubbed his paws together. "Excellent! That younger woman represents what we call your target audience. You'll write the book for her, and for her alone. She'll read the book, and she'll love it, because it gives her a powerful emotional experience. She'll tell other people about it, and some of them might like your book. But none of them will love it as much as she does. Is it okay with you if she's your biggest fan?"

"Oh, that would be wonderful!" Goldilocks said. "I know just how she feels and thinks."

Little Pig stood up and stamped loudly with his hooves on the tile floor. "That sounds like a terrible business decision," he said.

Baby Bear spun to look at him. "And why do you say that?" he asked politely.

"Modern business requires economies of scale," said Little Pig. "To make the highest possible profit, you need to move the maximum number of units at the lowest possible cost. That requires you to create products targeted to the lowest common denominator. That's how I made my fortune, and that's how I intend to write my book."

Baby Bear scratched his furry chin and looked at the class. "How many of you want your work to be read by millions?"

Every student in the room raised their hands.

"And what's the best-selling novel series of the last twenty years?" Baby Bear asked.

Mrs. Hubbard scowled. "It was those dreadful books about that Harvey Potter child. Witches and wizards and all sorts of wickedness."

"A very stupid book," growled Little Pig. "I stopped reading after the first page, when I saw how that woman maligned those respectable Dursleys."

"And who was the target audience for the Harry Potter series?" asked Baby Bear.

Nobody said anything.

Goldilocks timidly raised her hand. "Wasn't it ... eleven-year-old boys?"

Baby Bear began jumping up and down, clapping his fat little paws. "Yes! Boys, aged eleven. The smallest niche market you can imagine. Everybody knows that boys don't read. Everybody knows that eleven-year-old boys absolutely, positively won't read anything. Especially a book written by a woman. And yet ..."

"Harrumph!" Little Pig snorted. "Lots of people read the Harry Potter series. Although God only knows why anyone would read such nonsense."

Baby Bear scratched his ears. "The author wrote her books for a very tight niche market. Eleven-year-old boys. But she delighted those boys, and they talked about it to eleven-year-old girls. They were also delighted and talked about it to twelve-year-olds. Who talked about it to thirteen-year-olds. And so on, until everybody was talking about it. What made that work?"

"A wicked spell?" said Mrs. Hubbard.

"Great marketing of an inferior product," said Little Pig.

"Good writing that delighted her target audience?" said Goldilocks.

"Exactly!" said Baby Bear. "So when you go to write your story, you are not going to write for the whole world. You are going to choose your target audience and define it as tightly as you know how. You are going to write your story to delight your target audience. You will not care about anybody else."

"But what if other people ... hate my writing?" Goldilocks said. She couldn't bear the thought of anybody not liking her novel.

"You. Don't. Care." Baby Bear got so excited, he began running in tight little circles. "The only people in the world that you have to make happy are the people in your target audience. If everybody else hates it, you don't care."

"That's the biggest load of nonsense I've ever heard," said Little Pig.

"But … there were ever so many people who read Harvey Potter who weren't eleven-year-old boys!" said Mrs. Hubbard. "All sorts of folk who ought to have known better."

"That's my point!" said Baby Bear. "Here is your marketing plan, in three simple steps." He went to the whiteboard and began writing in large letters.

YOUR MARKETING PLAN

1) Choose the target audience you want to delight.

2) Write the best story you can, aiming exactly at that target audience.

3) When you publish your story, market it ONLY to your target audience.

4) Your target audience will tell the rest of the world.

"That is four steps," said Little Pig. "Apparently, bears can't count."

"But … *we* only have to do three of them," Goldilocks said. "The fourth step happens on its own. I took marketing in college. That fourth step is what all marketers dream about. It's called 'word of mouth.'"

Baby Bear jabbed his paw in the air. "Bazinga!" he shouted. "Every writer desperately wants word of mouth to take off for their book. That happens *only* if you delight your target audience. That happens *only* if you write a book precisely for your target audience. That happens *only* if you make a conscious decision from the beginning on who your target audience is."

The entire class went silent. Even Little Pig had nothing to say.

Baby Bear walked over to stand in front of Goldilocks. "Now, let's continue. Your target audience is who, exactly?"

"Women about my age," Goldilocks said, remembering what she had learned in college about demographics.

"Women your age read all sorts of novels. What sort of story *exactly* does your target audience like to read?"

"Exciting stories. Stories with something dangerous happening. There's a handsome hero and a beautiful heroine. And they're starting to fall in love, but they don't dare, because that will ruin the mission. But they fall in love anyway, because they can't help themselves. And there's an evil villain waiting to ruin them. And everything goes from bad to worse to horrible, and it looks like they can't possibly succeed in their mission, and even if they do, you just know that one of them will die tragically, and that would spoil their love story. And yet ..."

Goldilocks stopped. She knew it sounded very foolish.

"And yet, somehow, it all works out in the end," Baby Bear said.

"It might," said Goldilocks. "Or one of them might die tragically. Because my books will sometimes have a happy ending and sometimes a tragic ending, so you never know how *this* book will end until you get there."

Baby Bear spun to face the class. "How many of you would buy that kind of a book?"

A number of hands shot up around the room.

Mrs. Hubbard didn't raise her hand.

Neither did Little Pig.

Goldilocks felt horrible for a moment. Not everybody liked her kind of story. In fact, more than half of the people didn't like her kind of story.

"Marvelous!" said Baby Bear. "See how many people are in your target audience?"

Goldilocks thought that he sounded like one of those annoying glass-half-full kind of bears. Then she began looking at the people raising their hands. Some of them were the kind she had envisioned reading her story—young women like herself. But there were a couple of middle-aged men who liked her story. And a few older women. And some teens. She couldn't imagine what demographic group might possibly fit this motley crowd.

"I think you've got a great target audience," Baby Bear said. "You defined it by *what they like*, not by their age or their gender or their socioeconomic status. You gave me a *psychographic*, not a *demographic*."

Goldilocks felt her head spinning. Was everything she had learned in college all wrong? And why were they wasting time talking about *marketing* when what she really wanted to do was talk about *writing*?

Baby Bear looked at his watch. "We need to take a ten-minute break. When we come back, we'll continue with Goldilocks and her story. And I'll teach you how to develop the most powerful marketing tool you can ever have for your novel."

The students noisily went out of the room.

Goldilocks followed them, feeling terribly disappointed. She had spent all of college learning marketing, and she was bored to death of it. She wanted to learn how to write a novel, not market a novel. Perhaps her best bet would be to quietly sneak away and go home.

Chapter Three

YOUR STORY IN ONE SENTENCE

*B*ut Goldilocks found it impossible to sneak away. During the break, she was mobbed by other students, all asking her how long she had been writing and what were her secrets for being so brilliant.

Goldilocks had no idea what to tell them, so she sipped coffee and shrugged mysteriously. Even when she went to the ladies' room, she was surrounded by her new friends, who would not stop talking. She felt like a terrible fraud. If these writers learned that she had only written one word in her novel, they'd know she was nothing but an airhead.

When the class resumed, the room was buzzing with excitement.

Goldilocks felt like the world's biggest phony.

Baby Bear told Goldilocks to sit in the chair in front again, and then he began pacing in front of her.

"In our last session, we talked about your target audience—what kind of story delights them. And we imagined a specific young woman who happens to be in your target audience. Can you see her in your mind's eye?"

Goldilocks nodded. The young woman looked a lot like her.

Baby Bear was smiling. "Now this woman asks the store owner if there's anything good that she might like to read. And the owner takes her to your book and says that he has a new book that just arrived, and it's about … what?"

Goldilocks didn't know what to say. "It's a romantic suspense novel and she'll love it."

Baby Bear nodded slowly. "That's a good start. It's romantic suspense. But it's not enough to *tell* a customer she's going to love your book. You have to *show* her that she's going to love your book."

"Oh, well …" Goldilocks fanned her face. "How do I do that?"

"You give her a taste of the story in twenty-five words or less."

Goldilocks thought for a minute. "Okay, so my story's about this young woman living in France in World War II, and her husband went off to the war years ago and was killed, and she has a young daughter, and she's just scraping by growing roots and things in the garden, and she's horribly afraid the Nazis will take her daughter away because they'll say she's defective, and there's this nasty old Nazi sympathizer in the village who's been making advances to her, and she knows that if she turns him down, he might tell the Nazis about her daughter, but he's just so repulsive that she can't stand him, and when she complains to the mayor, he tells her that we all have to make hard choices, and—"

"Wasn't there a handsome young American agent parachuting into her life?" Baby Bear asked.

Goldilocks put her hands on her hips and glared at him. "I'm *getting* to that! But first I have to tell you all the things you need to know to understand my story."

Baby Bear looked out at the class. "How many of you need to know everything that Goldilocks just told you?"

A few students timidly raised their hands halfway.

Goldilocks couldn't understand why they had all lost enthusiasm. Fifteen minutes ago, they'd all thought her story sounded amazing.

"What you're telling us is called backstory," Baby Bear said. "We want to hear the real story."

"But … you *have* to know all this first," Goldilocks said.

"Did you ever read *The Day of the Jackal*, by Frederick Forsyth?" Baby Bear asked.

"Yes, a long time ago. I loved that book."

"What's it about?"

"Well, it's a thriller about a professional assassin hired by French terrorists to kill Charles de Gaulle."

Baby Bear was counting on his paws as he mumbled to himself. When he finished, he grinned at her and said, "Sixteen."

"What?" Goldilocks stared at him.

"You summarized the whole story in sixteen words. You told me the category and told me enough of the story to get me interested." Baby Bear turned to the students. "How many of you would buy that book right now if I had it here for sale?"

Six hands shot up.

"What's the title again?" shouted one student.

"Who's the author?" said another.

Baby Bear pointed at the six students with their hands up. "You people are in the target audience for *The Day of the Jackal*. Goldilocks just summarized the story in exactly the form you need in order to know that you would love the story. Well done!"

Goldilocks hung her head modestly. She hadn't done anything special. The story was a good one, and she'd just told the barest essentials.

"Now quickly," Baby Bear said. "For those six students who just raised their hands, how would you summarize your book?"

"Well, isn't it obvious?" Goldilocks couldn't believe that Baby Bear wasn't getting it. "I'm writing a romantic suspense novel about a woman in Nazi-occupied France who falls in love with an American saboteur on a mission to, um, do something really super horrible to the Nazis that will change the course of the war."

For a minute, there had been real tension hanging in the air.

But right after Goldilocks had said the word "um," the excitement seemed to drain out of the room in a whoosh.

Goldilocks made a mental note to never say "um" again.

Baby Bear was smiling though, pacing back and forth. "That was an excellent start. You told us the category. I can see the woman. I can see the saboteur. But I can't see his mission."

Goldilocks frowned at him. "It's really important. It's huge. It could change the war. Don't you get it?" She couldn't believe that the conference director would hire a teacher who had so little understanding of fiction.

Baby Bear shook his head. "You can *tell* me that it's important and huge and will change the war. But I don't feel any of that just because you told me. I have to reach that conclusion myself. So you have to *show* me it's huge and important."

"But ... in *The Day of the Jackal*, that's what happened. The assassin was going to shoot Charles de Gaulle, and that would have changed everything in France."

Baby Bear turned to the class. "How many of you can picture an assassin shooting Charles de Gaulle?"

Every hand in the room went up.

"How many of you can picture a man doing something really super horrible to the French government?"

All the hands went down.

Baby Bear looked at Goldilocks. "The act of shooting Charles de Gaulle is concrete. We can see him pull the trigger. We can hear the rifle shot. We can feel the boom. We can smell the gunpowder. And we know without you telling us that this is going to badly damage the French government."

"So ... what's your point?" Goldilocks asked.

"The act of 'doing something super horrible' is abstract. We can't see it, because there are a million super horrible things it could be, and they all look different. We can't hear it. We can't smell it. We can't feel it."

The class was silent for about ten seconds.

Goldilocks was so angry she wanted to stomp out of the room. Why was Baby Bear being so obtuse? "I keep telling you and you won't listen! I'm writing a romantic suspense novel about a woman in Nazi-occupied France who falls in love with an injured American saboteur who wants to blow up a key ammunition depot at Normandy just before D-Day."

All the students stood up and began cheering.

Baby Bear clapped his paws together and pranced around Goldilocks in a circle. "That sounds brilliant, Goldilocks."

Little Pig harrumphed. "That was thirty-five words. You said it had to be twenty-five words or less."

Mrs. Hubbard raised her hand. "Wouldn't it be better if you put in something about a cupboard?"

Baby Bear shook his head. "It could be a little shorter, Little Pig, but I think it works. And Mrs. Hubbard, this story has no cupboards. Goldilocks, I think you've nailed this one. You didn't *tell* us that the stakes are high. You *showed* us. If this saboteur blows up all the German ammo, then it hurts the Nazis badly. But if he fails, it could allow them to repel the coming invasion. Very good. There are consequences for both success *and* failure."

Goldilocks felt like her story had suddenly come into focus. She had known that her hero was on a mission to strike a terrible blow against the Nazis. But until she spelled out exactly what the mission was, her story had too many possible directions. Now she had fewer options, and she suddenly felt like this story would almost write itself.

Baby Bear stepped to the whiteboard and began writing:

YOUR ONE-SENTENCE SUMMARY

1) Give yourself one hour for this task.

2) Write one sentence that tells the following:

a) What category your book is.

b) Who your lead characters are.

c) What one thing they desperately want to do.

3) Don't tell any backstory.

4) Paint a picture for your target audience.

5) Be as short as possible, but no shorter.

Beneath that, he wrote Goldilocks's one-sentence summary:

A romantic suspense novel about a woman in Nazi-occupied France who falls in love with an injured American saboteur on a mission to blow up a key ammunition depot at Normandy just before D-Day.

He counted the words. "Thirty-six. I don't think you can make it shorter. Congratulations, Goldilocks. You're ready to move on to the next step in writing your novel."

Goldilocks felt confusion wash through her. "But … what does this have to do with writing? You said this is just a marketing tagline. Why aren't you teaching us how to write a novel?"

Baby Bear grinned at her. "The first person you have to market to is yourself. You have to be excited about your story. Which means you have to know what your story is. This is huge progress."

"But … I haven't written anything yet! All we have is one crummy sentence."

"It's a very good sentence, and it's one sentence more than you had an hour ago," Baby Bear said.

Little Pig stood up and cleared his throat, punching numbers furiously on a calculator. "At this rate, it will take you … 2,778 hours to write your novel. That's 116 straight days, if you work around the clock without eating or sleeping." He gave a sneer. "Whatever you think you're doing, Baby Bear, it isn't working."

Chapter Four

YOUR CREATIVE PARADIGM

Goldilocks had never felt so disappointed. She had worked very hard on her one-sentence summary. She felt in her heart that it was a good one. But it had taken a whole hour to write it. And she just didn't think she could stand writing the entire novel so slowly.

"Are you okay, Goldilocks?" Baby Bear said. "You don't look happy."

"I just …" Goldilocks put her head in her hands. "I don't know what you're doing, but it doesn't seem to be working. We've only got one sentence, and there are thousands more to write. We'll never get done at this rate."

Baby Bear started laughing. "Are you kidding? There are ten steps to writing a novel, and you've already finished the first one —and it only took an hour. You're doing wonderfully."

Goldilocks looked at the one sentence on the whiteboard. "I don't understand. You're telling me we're already a tenth of the way there? That can't be right."

Little Pig jabbed a hoof at Baby Bear. "You obviously don't know anything about writing. How many novels have you published, young bear?"

Baby Bear shrugged. "Half a dozen."

"Well, I've never heard of any of them." Little Pig peered at him through his wire-framed spectacles.

"There are millions of books in print, and hundreds of thousands of authors," Baby Bear said. "How many of those novels have you read, and how many authors can you name?"

Little Pig harrumphed. "I don't waste my time reading fiction, and—"

"And yet you want to write a novel?" Baby Bear said.

"Reading and writing are two different things," Little Pig said. "In any event, I don't have time to write the novel myself. I've worked out the story. I just need some clerical type to put it down on paper. Writers are a dime a dozen."

Goldilocks was getting rather tired of Little Pig. She stood up to her full height and glared at him. "Writing is skilled work, and if you think you can just hire a writer like you'd hire a gardener, then maybe your head isn't on straight. Now, if you don't mind, the rest of us came here to learn from Baby Bear, so why don't you sit down and listen?"

The whole class erupted in cheers.

Little Pig's face turned a bright pink. He spluttered and coughed and then sat down.

Baby Bear put his paw up to scratch his nose, but it didn't quite conceal the huge grin on his face. "We're overdue to talk about creative paradigms. Some of you have tried outlining your novel. How did that work out for you?"

A young man in the back raised his hand. "Outlining works pretty well for me."

The hipster woman next to him scowled furiously. "Outlining is horrible! It crushes the human spirit. You might just as well do a paint-by-numbers, because you aren't going to create great art by outlining."

Baby Bear held up his paws. "Peace, people. Outlining is a method that's proven to work for many authors. Many of you probably liked *The Bourne Identity*. The author of the novel, Robert Ludlum, was famous for his long and detailed outlines."

Goldilocks was trembling. "But ... I tried outlining and it didn't work."

Baby Bear just looked at her. "You tried it and it didn't work *for you*. Outlining is one example of what I call a 'creative paradigm.' It's a method for helping you write your first draft, and it works for some people. However, it doesn't work for everybody."

Goldilocks sighed deeply. She desperately needed a creative paradigm that worked for her.

"Another well-known creative paradigm is seat-of-the-pants writing," Baby Bear said. "You just sit down and write your novel with no idea where you're going. How many of you have tried that?"

The hipster woman in back said, "If you ask me, that's the only way you're going to get great art. You let your story well up from your inmost being."

The young man next to her gave a sneer. "That's just a load of crap. Which is about what you'd expect to well up from your inmost being."

The woman's face turned a brilliant red, and she looked like she was going to explode.

"Please," Baby Bear said in a calming tone. "Seat-of-the-pants writing is another example of a creative paradigm, and it works wonderfully well for some authors. Stephen King is a famous seat-of-the-pants writer. But again, it doesn't work for everybody."

Goldilocks couldn't stand it any longer. "Why don't you quit beating around the bush? You've got your own creative paradigm and it works for everybody, so let's just hear it, shall we?"

Baby Bear shook his head. "Well, that's just the problem. I've got a creative paradigm that works well for me, and for tens of thousands of other writers, but it doesn't work for everybody.

There isn't any creative paradigm that works for everybody. What I'm trying to explain is that you will each have to find the creative paradigm that works best for you, and then ignore all the others."

"But ... hadn't you better get started?" Goldilocks said. "You've wasted all this time teaching us about our target audience and our one-sentence summary. When are you going to teach us your creative paradigm?"

"Actually, we're well under way," Baby Bear said. "My creative paradigm is called the Snowflake Method, and you've completed the first step—writing the one-sentence summary. There are only ten steps, and we're ready to work on step 2. But first, who knows why it's called the Snowflake Method?"

Nobody said anything.

"I suppose I'll have to show you." Baby Bear tapped the power switch on the PowerPoint projector on the table.

The back wall lit up, showing the display on his laptop. The only thing on the screen was a large image of a snowflake:

Baby Bear tugged Goldilocks to the whiteboard and handed her a marker. "I want you to draw that picture of a snowflake in one continuous stroke—without lifting the marker or erasing."

Goldilocks studied the image. "I can't. That's too hard. I could never do that. It's impossible. However did you draw that?"

Baby Bear grinned. "Actually, I didn't. I wrote a computer program to draw that."

"Well, it's incredibly complicated! It must be a very long program."

"No, it's a very short program, and it uses exactly the same procedure that a human or a bear can use to draw that image. Let me show you how it works." Baby Bear took a marker and drew three straight lines on the whiteboard to make a triangle.

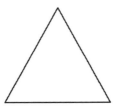

"That doesn't look a bit like a snowflake," Goldilocks said. "You aren't anywhere near done yet."

"I didn't say I was done." Baby Bear erased the central third of each of the straight lines and added the two edges for each of three smaller triangles so that he now had a six-pointed star.

Goldilocks put her hands on her hips. "It still doesn't look much like a snowflake. And anyway, you cheated. You lifted your marker *and* you erased lines."

Baby Bear just looked at her. "Who said I couldn't erase lines or lift my marker?"

"You did." Goldilocks turned to the class. "Didn't he say I couldn't erase the lines?"

Everybody nodded.

Baby Bear chortled. "And you *believed* me? Just because I said you had to do it that way, you believed me? Even though it makes it harder, you just accepted that you should do it that way?"

Goldilocks didn't know what to say, so she just glared at him.

Baby Bear hopped up on the table next to his laptop and pointed at the class. "This is important, you novelists! You're going to get lots of advice on how to write a novel. But that's all it is. *Advice.* If you don't like that advice, if it doesn't work for you, then ignore it. If it does work for you, then run with it."

"But ..." Goldilocks spluttered. "These teachers at the conference know what they're talking about, don't they?"

"They know what works for them," Baby Bear said. "But they don't know what works for you. If they advise you to write an outline like Robert Ludlum and it doesn't work for you, then what do you do?"

"Um ... cry?" Goldilocks said.

"No! Ignore the advice!" Baby Bear's furry little face was turning red. "And if they advise you to write seat-of-the-pants like Stephen King and it doesn't work for you, then what do you do?"

"But ... that's supposed to be 'organic,'" Goldilocks said. "How can 'organic' be wrong?"

Baby Bear began hopping up and down in rage. "Organic?" he bellowed. "What a load of nonsense! There's nothing organic about seat-of-the-pants writing! It's a method of writing. It works for some great writers. It doesn't work for other great writers. So what do you do if it doesn't work for you?"

"Find something that does?" Goldilocks said.

"Exactly." Baby Bear grabbed the marker and went back to the whiteboard. "If you're a great artist, you can draw this snowflake seat-of-the-pants with one continuous motion, never erasing. But very few people are great artists. They can draw something in one continuous motion, but it's going to come out all warped and lopsided, and they're going to have to erase huge pieces of it and keep trying over and over, until they get it right."

"Don't great writers write dozens and dozens of drafts of their novel until they get it right?" Goldilocks said.

Baby Bear laughed. "Yes, if they're seat-of-the-pants writers. They have to. But Snowflakers don't. Just let me finish drawing my snowflake, and you'll see why."

He erased smaller pieces from each of the straight lines on his six-pointed star. Then he added in smaller triangles.

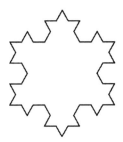

Goldilocks thought it was finally starting to look like a snowflake. It wasn't finished, but she could see where it was going.

Baby Bear did another round of changes, and now it was really looking like a snowflake.

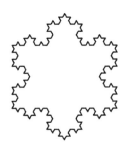

He did one more round, and then he stepped back. "How does it look?"

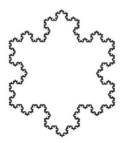

Goldilocks gasped. "It looks … perfect."

"It's perfect at each stage, but it's always incomplete," Baby Bear said. "You can keep going like that forever. This is a mathematical object called a snowflake fractal, and you can prove that the length of its perimeter is infinite."

"But after you've done a few of those rounds, it's as good as you can get with that thick marker you're using," Goldilocks said. "Once the length of each edge is less than the width of the marker, making more changes won't help."

"Exactly!" Baby Bear said. "But notice this. The first round of revisions was very simple. I erased parts of three edges and drew in a few lines. The second round was a little more complicated. The third round was more complicated yet."

"But at every stage, it was nice and symmetrical," Goldilocks said. "It was perfect, but not finished."

Baby Bear smiled. "If I had drawn this 'organically,' it would never be perfect at any stage. And I'd always be making huge fixes to different parts of it."

"That's really dumb," Goldilocks said. "Who would draw it that way?"

"What you mean is that it would be dumb for you," Baby Bear said. "Because it makes sense to you to draw it the way I just showed you. But a seat-of-the-pants artist would hate drawing it my way."

"Then … who's right?" Goldilocks asked. "What's the one best way of drawing the snowflake?"

"The one that works for you," Baby Bear said. "And what did I tell you about the different methods of writing a novel?"

"Always use the method of writing that works for you," Goldilocks said.

"Exactly." Baby Bear put the marker down and dusted his paws. "Now are you ready for the second stage of the Snowflake Method of writing a novel?"

Goldilocks shook her head. "It just sounds too simple. You make it sound like anybody could write a novel. That can't be right. Creating great art should be painful. Everybody knows that."

Baby Bear's phone buzzed. He took it out, read a text message, then tapped on it for a few seconds and put it away. "Well, Goldilocks, you've tried outlining, and it didn't work for you. You've tried seat-of-the-pants writing, and it didn't work for you. What do you have to lose by trying the Snowflake Method?"

Goldilocks was getting rather tired of Baby Bear's logical approach to everything.

The door suddenly flew open with a tremendous bang.

A large, evil-looking wolf wearing a mask rushed into the room. He pointed a huge handgun at Baby Bear and fired.

Baby Bear grabbed his chest.

Blood squirted out.

Goldilocks screamed.

Baby Bear fell to the floor and lay still.

Chapter Five

THE IMPORTANCE OF BEING DISASTROUS

The Big Bad Wolf pointed his gun at Goldilocks. "What's this I hear about you wanting to use the Snowflake Method? If you do, I'll make it painful for you. Very painful."

Goldilocks felt a rush of heat in her veins. He had no right! She put her head down and ran directly at the Big Bad Wolf, spearing him in the stomach.

The Big Bad Wolf flew backward and hit the floor with a giant "oomph!"

Goldilocks landed on top of him, punching, kicking, biting, scratching, and screaming. She sat on his stomach and pinned his paws on each side of his head. "Somebody grab his gun!"

"Hey, take it easy, Blondie!" said the Big Bad Wolf. "I can explain."

"You killed Baby Bear!" Goldilocks bellowed. "And now you want me to take it easy?"

"I didn't … kill anyone," said the Big Bad Wolf, grunting for breath.

A furry paw settled on Goldilocks's shoulder.

She spun her head to look.

Baby Bear stood there grinning. "I'm fine. This is my friend, the Big Bad Wolf. I asked him to burst in and fire a blank at me. I had a capsule of fake blood in my paw, and I smashed it on my chest."

Goldilocks was so surprised, she couldn't think. "You'd better get that fur in cold water right away or the blood is never going to come out."

The Big Bad Wolf wriggled underneath her. "Hey, Blondie, no offense, but you're kind of heavy, and you're sitting on my stomach."

Goldilocks felt very foolish sitting on the wolf, so she stood up. She scowled and jabbed a finger at Baby Bear. "What is the meaning of all this? You two scared me to death with your horrible stunt."

Baby Bear went down on one knee and took Goldilocks's hand in his soft paw. "I'm very sorry. I wanted to teach you something, and that was the best way I knew to do it. Will you forgive me?"

Goldilocks didn't know what to say. Her insides were all in a tizzy. She felt hot and angry and frightened and embarrassed, all at the same time.

The Big Bad Wolf stood up and dusted himself off, then pressed a paw carefully into his belly. "Humans have very hard heads, did you know that?"

Goldilocks realized she could have hurt the Big Bad Wolf very badly. "I'm sorry. I … thought you had killed Baby Bear. And I thought you were going to kill me."

"Why would I kill you?" the Big Bad Wolf asked. A sly smile slid across his face. "I said I'd shoot you only if you decided to use the Snowflake Method."

"Because …" Goldilocks didn't realize she'd made the decision until she thought about it just now. "Because when you threatened me, when you said I couldn't use the Snowflake Method, I realized that … I really do want to try it out."

"Bazinga!" shouted Baby Bear. He leaped up in the air and began dancing around in a small circle, pumping his paws in the air like he'd scored a touchdown. He raced toward the table, leaped in the air, did a double flip, and landed on top, spinning to face the students. "Did everybody see what just happened there? Goldilocks made a decision."

All the students were staring at him with their mouths hanging open.

The Big Bad Wolf went to the whiteboard and picked up a marker. He held it poised at the board and wrote:

WHY YOUR STORY NEEDS DISASTERS
   1.
   2.
   3.

Baby Bear said, "In your story, you must have disasters. Big, horrible, hairy disasters. Where people get hurt, possibly. Or somebody threatens to hurt them. Why?"

"Because … it's exciting?" Goldilocks said.

The Big Bad Wolf wrote:

---

1. EXCITEMENT

"Yes," Baby Bear said. "It's exciting to see one of your favorite bears get killed. But excitement is not enough. What else does a disaster do?"

Goldilocks mentally reviewed the sequence of events. The Big Bad Wolf had shot Baby Bear. Then he had threatened her with the same. And it had forced her to see what was important to her. Just before he was shot, Baby Bear had been asking her whether she wanted to use the Snowflake Method. She had waffled. But once the Big Bad Wolf told her she *couldn't*, she saw very clearly how much she wanted to.

"What else does a disaster do?" Baby Bear asked again.

"It ... forced me to make a decision," Goldilocks said.

The Big Bad Wolf wrote:

---

2. DECISION

"Exactly." Baby Bear did a double backflip off the table and landed in Goldilocks's arms. He planted a furry kiss on her cheek.

Goldilocks wasn't sure how she felt about that. She really didn't want bear germs on her face, but she squeezed Baby Bear in a big hug because she realized that she liked him very much, even if he was a bear, and a silly one at that. She set him down on the floor. "But ... why do I need to make decisions?"

The Big Bad Wolf grinned. "Because it sends your story in a new direction. It keeps things interesting. Otherwise, your story would start feeling like it's all alike." He wrote:

---

3. NEW DIRECTIONS

Baby Bear began pacing back and forth. "Your reader wants all of those things. Excitement. Decisions. New directions. And they want those on a regular schedule. Which means you need to schedule them. If you imagine your story is like a football game, then you need a major disaster at the end of the first quarter, and another one right at halftime, and another at the end of the third quarter."

"But ... why?" Goldilocks said. "Do you have to?"

Baby Bear shook his head. "You don't have to do anything. But if you look at stories that work, stories that move people's emotions, they're often divided into four parts, with a major disaster between each part."

The Big Bad Wolf raised his paw. "Like in *Star Wars*," he said. "At the end of the first quarter, Luke's aunt and uncle get killed by the stormtroopers and he decides to join Obi-Wan Kenobi in the Rebellion."

"Right," Baby Bear said. "Then at halftime, Obi-Wan Kenobi duels with Darth Vader using lightsabers, and Vader kills him. Now *that's* a disaster, and it forces Luke to become his own man, to quit depending on his mentor."

Goldilocks was starting to see it. "And then, when they get to the rebel planet, they learn that the Death Star has been tracking them, and it's coming to destroy the rebel planet. So now they have to decide—will they run and hide, or stand and fight?"

Baby Bear nodded. "That's an especially important decision. They decide to stand and fight, which means that there are only two possible endings. Either they are all going to die, or the Death Star will be destroyed. The third disaster *forces* the ending. It's a beautifully structured story."

Goldilocks felt skeptical. Baby Bear's pattern worked for big, exciting stories with lots of explosions. But she didn't think it would work for romance novels, and she read a lot of those. "There aren't people getting shot in *Pride and Prejudice*," she said.

The Big Bad Wolf laughed loudly at that. "She's got you there, Baby Bear! From what I hear, *Pride and Prejudice* is one of those boring books where no planets explode, nobody gets killed, and there's not even a lightsaber in sight. How can you have a disaster without any of those?"

Baby Bear frowned. *"Pride and Prejudice* is a romance story between Lizzie Bennet and Mr. Darcy, correct?"

Goldilocks nodded. "And a romance is simple. Boy meets girl. Boy loses girl. Boy gets girl. So where are your three disasters? I only see one disaster—boy loses girl."

The Big Bad Wolf shook his head sadly. "Baby Bear, your theory has more holes than a swiss cheese sandwich."

Baby Bear reached into his backpack and pulled out an iPad. He tapped on it several times and began scanning the screen furiously, muttering to himself.

Goldilocks felt horrible. She was embarrassing poor Baby Bear in front of his class.

Finally Baby Bear looked up. "Very well, then. Right at the one-quarter mark in the story, Lizzie Bennet is talking to her good friend Mr. Wickham, and he tells her that Mr. Darcy financially ruined him for no good reason. What would you call that?"

"Boy loses girl," Goldilocks said. "I'll grant you that's a disaster, but you need two more."

Baby Bear flicked his paw across the screen, turning pages rapidly. "Halfway through the story, Mr. Darcy asks Lizzie to marry him. And she says …?"

Goldilocks felt her heart lurch. "She says that he is the last man she would ever be prevailed upon to marry."

The Big Bad Wolf rubbed his large paws together. "Uh-oh! Did she use the F-word on him? Did she say, 'forever?' Because if she did, she means business. I haven't read the story, but it sounds like boy loses girl *permanently."*

Baby Bear kept flipping pages. "Turning to the end of the third quarter, Lizzie is just starting to get to know Mr. Darcy, and she realizes that he's a pretty decent man, but then her sister Lydia runs off to live in sin with Mr. Wickham, who has turned out to be a liar and cheat. What would you call that?"

Goldilocks felt very small. "It sounds like another disaster. The worst one yet."

"Yow! Sounds like girl loses boy this time," said the Big Bad Wolf. "If Lizzie's family has a scandal, Mr. Darcy can't possibly marry her, right?"

Goldilocks shook her head. "You need to read more books, Big Bad Wolf. Yes, that's a disaster, but it forces Mr. Darcy to do something kind and noble—he pays Mr. Wickham's debts and makes him marry Lydia and so the family's honor is restored. And he does it in secret, but Lizzie finds out and realizes that she's been in love with him the whole time. And they live happily ever after."

The Big Bad Wolf looked shocked. "Really? That sounds cool! I had no idea a book about dusty old people could be so … interesting." He grabbed Baby Bear's iPad and sat down in a corner and began reading.

Baby Bear looked at Goldilocks. "Now you know enough about story structure to work on the second step of the Snowflake for your story. You've got this American saboteur and he's landed in the garden of a nice French woman and he's broken his leg. She's taking care of him. What goes wrong?"

Goldilocks thought for a second. "The mean old Nazi sympathizer comes to court our heroine and … sees the American soldier."

"That's a disaster," Baby Bear said. "And what decision does she make? What's going to change the course of the story?"

Goldilocks began jumping up and down. "She decides to protect the American. Up till now, she's been terrified, thinking that she has to turn the American in to the Nazis. But when this awful man threatens to turn her in, she kills him right there. Then she and the American bury him in the yard."

"That's a good disaster and a huge decision," Baby Bear said. "So now she's committed to the story. It's like when Luke joined the Rebellion in *Star Wars*. Once he does that, he can't turn back. Your heroine can't turn back either—she can't unkill the collaborator."

"But now it's going to be horrible for her," Goldilocks said. "People might find out she killed that man, and then she'll be in real trouble."

"That's *her* problem, not yours," Baby Bear said. "*You* have the opposite problem. What if *nobody* finds out she killed the collaborator?"

"Then ... she'll be fine and the American will be perfectly safe," Goldilocks said.

"That's bad," Baby Bear said. "Horrible! You can't leave your characters being safe. Safe is boring."

Goldilocks shook her head. "You don't understand, Baby Bear. She can't do something stupid. She has to try to act as if nothing happened. She has to play safe. She has to protect her daughter."

"Exactly," Baby Bear said. "Your heroine naturally will try to play safe. But you, the novelist, will never play safe. What's the worst thing in the world that could happen to your heroine?"

"The Nazis could take her daughter because she's supposedly 'defective.'"

"Perfect," said Baby Bear. "That might just work as your second disaster. The Nazis could take her daughter. But explain to us why they think she's 'defective.'"

"She has Down syndrome. She's eight years old, but she has the mind of a four-year-old."

"Aha!" said Baby Bear. "And so she's old enough to know about this American man in the house and about the collaborator who was killed, but she's not old enough to be a good liar."

Goldilocks sat down on the floor with her head in her hands. "This is horrible. My poor, poor heroine. She's been trying so hard to be safe, and now the worst has happened."

"No, this is wonderful," Baby Bear said. "She'll have to stop being safe and start doing scary things. What scary thing is she going to do first?"

Goldilocks felt like she was going to throw up. She imagined what she would do if the Nazis took her own daughter and were going to send her to a death camp. That would be too terrible for words. Tears sprang up in her eyes. "She's going to … intercept the truck taking her daughter off to the concentration camp and kill the Nazis driving it and get her daughter back."

"All alone?" said Baby Bear. "Won't she need help?"

"She's got this American man, and he's become her lover, and he loves her daughter. He'll help her. He'll do anything for her. His lower leg is in a cast, but he can walk, and he has weapons."

"So what's the plan?" Baby Bear said. "This is promising, but they need a plan."

"Well, I suppose they'll set up an ambush for the truck and kill the driver and the soldiers and … rescue the daughter and live happily ever after."

Baby Bear slumped to the floor with his head in his paws. "No, no, no. That's too easy. And it's too soon. You need another disaster. And isn't D-Day coming?"

Goldilocks felt like her head was spinning. "Yes, it's Saturday night, and our hero knows that D-Day will most likely be Monday, Tuesday, or Wednesday."

Baby Bear gave her an odd look. "They didn't have D-Day all planned out months in advance?"

Goldilocks frowned at him. "You don't know much about history, do you? The Allies needed moonlight at night for the paratroopers and a low tide at dawn for the attack. That gave them a three-day window in early June. They almost launched the invasion on Monday, but bad weather made them delay twenty-four hours."

Baby Bear was grinning. "It sounds like you've done your homework on this."

"Well, of course. But as I was saying, D-Day is almost upon them, and our hero hasn't blown up the ammunition dump that he was supposed to. And now he can't, because he has to help the heroine."

Baby Bear just looked at her. "You're a novelist, Goldilocks. There's no such thing as 'can't.' *Make* it work."

Goldilocks felt sweat sliding down her sides. "So they set up an ambush and kill the driver of the truck and the soldiers, but the American is wounded. Oh dear … I'm afraid he's fatally wounded." She shook her head and wiped her eyes. "This is horrible. What a terrible thing to happen."

"A disaster?" Baby Bear said. "And how does that lead to an ending?"

"Well, now they have a truck and the American is in terrible pain, but he puts on the Nazi driver's uniform and he and the heroine and the daughter drive to the ammo depot. He's brought his explosives."

"They have a frightening series of adventures along the way, I hope," said Baby Bear.

"Oh yes, but the poor man is bleeding and the heroine is crying and the daughter has to do the driving part of the way. And they finally reach the place at 3:00 a.m., and I don't know how they do it, but they get inside and blow it sky high."

Baby Bear smiled. "You don't have to know how they do it. That's for you to figure out later. But that's the ending. It's a sad ending and a happy ending, mixed together. I think that might work."

"That totally works," said the Big Bad Wolf from the corner, where he was madly flipping pages on the iPad. "Lots of killing. Lots of kissing. Sounds like a howling good story to me."

Baby Bear went to the whiteboard and found an empty space. "What we've learned is called the Three-Act Structure, although I sometimes like to call it the Three-Disaster Structure. Designing your Three-Act Structure is the second step of the Snowflake Method, and I like to do it in one paragraph of five sentences." He wrote on the board:

YOUR ONE-PARAGRAPH SUMMARY

1) Give yourself one hour for this task.

2) Write one paragraph with five sentences as follows:

a) Explain the setting and introduce the lead characters.

b) Explain the first quarter of the book, up to the first disaster, where the hero commits to the story.

c) Explain the second quarter of the book, up to the second disaster, where the hero changes his mode of operations.

d) Explain the third quarter of the book, up to the third disaster, which forces the hero to commit to the ending.

e) Explain the fourth quarter of the book, where the hero has the final confrontation and either wins or loses or both.

3) Focus on the disasters and the decisions that follow.

4) Don't try to figure out how you'll solve all the problems. Leave that for later. You only care about the big picture in this step.

Below this, he wrote Goldilocks's one-paragraph summary:

Ms. X is a young widow in Nazi-occupied France, and Mr. Y is an American saboteur who parachutes into her backyard and breaks his leg, three weeks before D-Day. Ms. X cares for Mr. Y and tries to decide whether to turn him in to the authorities, until the evil Mr. Z discovers them, and Ms. X is forced to kill him. Mr. Y helps Ms. X bury the body and she decides she must protect him, but then her 'defective' daughter is taken by the Nazis. Ms. X persuades Mr. Y to help ambush the transport, and they rescue her daughter, but Mr. Y has been fatally wounded. They drive the truck to the ammo depot,

evading Nazis all the way, and blow it up just in the nick of time
before the Allied invasion begins.

"How does that look?" Baby Bear said.

"I'd read that," said the Big Bad Wolf.

Goldilocks studied it for a moment and saw that there was something very, very wrong with it.

Chapter Six

NOTHING IS MORE IMPORTANT THAN CHARACTERS

"You don't look happy, Goldilocks," said Baby Bear. "Whatever is the matter? You've got a well-structured story with three acts. You have three disasters that escalate to a strong conclusion. What more could you want?"

Goldilocks sat on the floor and put her face in her hands and shook her head. "These people … they feel so flat!" She felt horrible for sounding ungrateful, but she couldn't help herself. Baby Bear was ruining her story.

"Explain what you mean by flat," Baby Bear said.

Goldilocks tried desperately to find the right words. "I … wanted a handsome man who's big and strong and kind. I wanted a beautiful heroine who's brave and fierce and passionate. And I don't see any of that here. This is going to be one of those awful, shoot-em-up stories where I don't care about the characters."

The Big Bad Wolf came over and patted her clumsily on the shoulder. "You want to tell her, Baby Bear, or shall I?" His voice sounded very kind.

Baby Bear sat down next to her on the floor. "The Snowflake Method has ten steps, and we've only looked at two. The third step is all about your characters."

A surge of hope rose in Goldilocks's heart. "R-really? We're going to work on my characters?"

"*You're* going to work on your characters," Baby Bear said. "I'll just make some suggestions on what to work on next."

"Good, because I don't want you writing my story for me. I'm the author, not you."

Baby Bear nodded. "Of course. You're the writer. You bring the creativity. The Snowflake Method just tells you what to be creative on next. And right now, it's time to get creative on your characters."

Baby Bear stood up and took Goldilocks's hand to pull her to her feet. "The first thing we need to do is make a list of your characters and give them roles and names." He went to the whiteboard and erased everything on it with the back of his furry paw. "Who is your lead character?"

Goldilocks sat on the edge of the table with her back to the other students. "My heroine. And her name is Elise. I like that name. I think it's pretty."

Baby Bear wrote down on the whiteboard, HEROINE: ELISE. "Very good. And you have a handsome hero, right?"

"Yes. He's from America, and his name is …" Goldilocks thought for a moment. "Dirk. That sounds strong and mysterious and a little dangerous. He's a brave soldier and he had a hard life growing up, so people think he's rough and a little cruel, but inside, he's kind and gentle."

Baby Bear wrote down, HERO: DIRK. "And Elise has a little daughter?"

"Yes, she's eight years old and her name is Monique."

Baby Bear wrote down, DAUGHTER: MONIQUE. "Now, there was this wretched French collaborator."

Goldilocks shrugged. "He's the villain, so I haven't thought much about him. He's just this wicked, evil man who wants to get Elise into bed, and he's collaborating with the Nazis because he's a coward. I hate him."

Baby Bear's small, furry mouth pursed into a thin, straight line. "Does this man have a name?"

Goldilocks shrugged. "It doesn't matter. Call him anything. He's awful."

Baby Bear just looked at her.

"Okay, call him Henri." Goldilocks wondered what had got into Baby Bear. He looked very worried about something.

Baby Bear wrote, VILLAIN: HENRI. "Are there any more main characters?"

Goldilocks couldn't think of any more. "There will be some minor characters. There's the village postmistress and the mayor and the Nazi soldiers. But they don't have big roles."

"Very well, then," Baby Bear said, still not smiling. "Now I need to know a bit more about these characters."

"Well, Elise is petite and pretty. And she has long, raven-black hair, beautiful and straight." Goldilocks fingered her curly blonde hair. "And green eyes. That's very important."

"Green eyes." Baby Bear sighed deeply. "That's it?"

"Blue eyes are so overdone."

"And what does Elise want?" Baby Bear said. "Specifically and concretely, what does she want most when the story begins?"

Goldilocks hadn't thought about that. "I don't know. She wants what every beautiful young woman wants, I suppose."

"And what is that?"

Goldilocks suddenly wondered why the room was so hot. She tried to think, but her head felt like it was packed with helium. Then she remembered the last Miss America contest. She'd felt so jealous of all those poised, beautiful, talented, intelligent young women. And every one of them wanted the exact same thing.

"World peace!" Goldilocks shouted. "Elise wants world peace!"

Baby Bear rolled his eyes.

The Big Bad Wolf fell to the floor, holding his stomach and laughing hysterically.

The whole class began giggling.

Goldilocks wondered what was so funny. World peace was important, wasn't it? Everybody knew that. Why wouldn't a young French woman, caught in World War II, want world peace?

Baby Bear sighed and pulled out his phone and a hundred-dollar bill. "Goldilocks, how long can you hold your breath?"

"I don't know. Maybe thirty seconds. It's been a long time since I tried."

"I'll give you this hundred-dollar bill if you can hold your breath for two minutes."

Goldilocks didn't know if she could do that, but it couldn't hurt to try. "Okay."

Baby Bear set the timer on his phone. "The Big Bad Wolf will squeeze your nose to make sure you don't cheat. If you open your mouth before the time's up, you lose."

Goldilocks nodded.

The Big Bad Wolf came over and gripped her nostrils tightly. "Is that comfortable, my dear?"

"It's fine."

"Take a deep breath and hold it," Baby Bear said.

Goldilocks filled her lungs and clamped her mouth shut.

Baby Bear started the timer.

The first fifteen seconds went comfortably, and Goldilocks thought this wasn't so hard. By thirty seconds, her lungs were starting to feel a little tight. At forty-five seconds, her head began feeling funny. As the timer passed one minute, she started feeling desperate.

Seconds ticked by, each more horrible than the last.

A minute and five seconds.

A minute six.

Goldilocks saw that she wasn't going to make it.

Her lungs were screaming for air.

She couldn't stand it any longer.

She opened her mouth and sucked in air.

The Big Bad Wolf released her nose and shook his head sadly. "Nice try, but no Benjamin."

Baby Bear put the hundred back in the little wallet clipped to his belt. "Why did you open your mouth?"

"Because I wanted air."

"Not world peace?"

Goldilocks giggled. "Not right then. I wanted air more than anything in the world."

"So why were you holding your breath?"

"Well … I also wanted that hundred-dollar bill."

Baby Bear burst into a smile. "That's what I call a Goal—when you want something specific and concrete. Like holding your breath for two minutes to earn a hundred dollars. You wanted that a lot, didn't you?"

Goldilocks nodded. "Well, of course. Very much."

"But you gave up."

"I suppose I just didn't want it enough."

"If it was a million dollars, do you think you could have lasted two minutes?"

"Maybe. I'd try a lot harder for a million dollars."

Baby Bear went to the whiteboard and wrote down:

PROPERTIES OF GOALS:
    Simple
    Concrete
    Important
    Achievable
    Difficult

The Big Bad Wolf was studying Goldilocks. "Would you really hold your breath for two minutes for a million dollars?"

Goldilocks thought about that. "It might take some training, but yes, I would."

"You'd like to be rich someday, wouldn't you?"

"Well … of course. Wouldn't everybody?"

The Big Bad Wolf shook his head. "No, of course not! What would a wolf do with money? Now if you offered me my own herd of little pigs—"

"Oh!" Goldilocks said. "That's horrible!"

"Objection!" squeaked Little Pig.

Baby Bear cleared his throat sharply. "Enough joking about pigs, Big Bad Wolf. That's not funny."

"Sorry." The Big Bad Wolf didn't sound very sorry.

"So you want to be rich, Goldilocks?" Baby Bear said.

She nodded.

"That's a bit abstract, isn't it? How would you know when you're rich?"

"Well … I don't know. But if I had a million dollars, I'd for sure be rich."

Baby Bear grinned. "Being rich is abstract. For one person, being rich means having a million dollars. For another, it means having a herd of little, um, cows. For a very poor person in a third-world country, it might mean owning a phone."

Goldilocks hadn't thought about any of that. "It's kind of like world peace, isn't it? That's vague and undefined too."

"Yes, world peace is an abstract idea," Baby Bear said. "That doesn't mean it's wrong to want world peace. But it does mean that you have to define what it means to you. You can't have a story about somebody who is trying to achieve world peace. You *can* have a story about somebody who's trying to eliminate all nuclear weapons from the planet. That's a Goal—it's simple, concrete, important, difficult, and just possibly achievable."

The Big Bad Wolf licked his lips. "A herd of little pigs is achievable."

"I'm going to speak to the conference director about this …

criminal!" Little Pig stomped out of the room.

Baby Bear smacked the Big Bad Wolf's paws. "That was very rude. After this workshop, you are going to go apologize to Little Pig. Is that clear?"

The Big Bad Wolf shot a venomous look at the door. "I *suppose.*"

Goldilocks wondered what this was all about. She thought that this couldn't be the first time the Big Bad Wolf had met Little Pig. There was obviously some bad blood between them, but she couldn't think what it might be about. The Big Bad Wolf didn't really want to eat Little Pig, did he? She shuddered.

Baby Bear was looking very angry. Finally, he turned back to Goldilocks. "I'm sorry, Goldilocks. Let's get back to your story. Something abstract like world peace is what I call an Ambition. It drives your Goal."

"I don't understand," Goldilocks said.

"You have an Ambition to be rich," Baby Bear said. "Therefore, if you had a chance to earn a million dollars by holding your breath for two minutes, you would make it your Goal to earn that million dollars. Because your Ambition is to be rich."

The Big Bad Wolf sneered. "I don't understand humans and their obsession with money, when what really matters is … um, food."

Goldilocks grabbed his shoulders and shook him hard. "How could you be so cruel to those poor pigs?"

"Because I like not being hungry," said the Big Bad Wolf. "How could you be so foolish as to want a big stack of green pieces of paper? What good is paper?"

"Because I can use money to buy anything I like. Such as clothes."

"Don't need those," said the Big Bad Wolf.

"Makeup."

"Don't need that either."

"A nice house."

"Not as good as a warm, dry cave."

"Food."

"That's what I said, but then you got all hoity-toity." The Big Bad Wolf scowled at her. "Don't you like bacon for breakfast?"

"That's different," said Goldilocks.

"How is that different?"

Baby Bear was jumping up and down with excitement. "Do you two see what you're arguing about?"

Goldilocks shook her head.

The Big Bad Wolf grinned and nodded.

"Values!" said Baby Bear. "Each of you values different things. Goldilocks values clothes and makeup and a nice house and food. That's what drives her Ambition to be rich someday—because then she'll have the things she values."

"Hmmph!" said the Big Bad Wolf. "Human Values make no sense at all. I'm happy with food."

"And a warm, dry cave," said Baby Bear.

"Well … of course."

Goldilocks shuddered. "Yuck, that would be horrible! How could you value a cave?"

The Big Bad Wolf shuddered back. "How could you value a huge, ugly, artificial house made of wood and plaster and stucco, reeking of unnatural things like paint and carpet and curtains? And keeping out the clean, fresh air and the moonlight? How would you even howl at night? That would be a horrible life."

"That will be enough arguing," said Baby Bear. "You two will be going round and round all day because each of you believes that your Values are 'obvious.' But they're only obvious to you. They're not obvious to everyone."

Goldilocks folded her arms across her chest. "My Values are obvious to anyone with a lick of sense."

The Big Bad Wolf scowled at her. "Your Values don't make any sense at all to animals. And there are more of us than there are of you."

"Time out!" Baby Bear shouted. "You'll never get anywhere by arguing about your Values. By definition, Values are so obvious that they can't be proved. Let's look at how this works." He went to the whiteboard and wrote down:

VALUES => AMBITION => GOAL

"Each one of us has Values that we think are obvious. Goldilocks believes that nothing is more important than money. The Big Bad Wolf thinks that nothing is more important than a herd of ... food. Neither of them can give a reason for their Values, because it seems to them that no reason is necessary. Their Values are Values because they just are."

"Obviously," Goldilocks said.

"Axiomatically," said the Big Bad Wolf.

Baby Bear grinned. "At least you two agree on something. And from your Values spring Ambitions. Because Goldilocks has a Value that nothing is more important than money, she has an Ambition to be rich someday. Her Value drives her Ambition. But that Ambition is abstract. We don't know what it looks like. Now if she has an opportunity to win a million dollars by holding her breath for two minutes, that creates a Goal for her—to win the money. That Goal would fulfill her Ambition to be rich."

The Big Bad Wolf gave a curt nod. "You could write a story about that—a greedy, blonde, airheaded girl who was willing to endanger her life to accumulate a large number of pieces of useless green paper."

Goldilocks scowled at him. "And the villain would be a large, smelly, pig-eating canine who tried to discourage the heroine from achieving her life's Ambition."

Baby Bear put his paws on his round, furry hips. "You two need to stop squabbling. Goldilocks, I'm going to give you homework. Are you ready to work on your characters and make them into real, human, three-dimensional people?"

She nodded and shot a sidelong glance at the Big Bad Wolf. "As long as they're *human*."

"A fate worse than death," muttered the Big Bad Wolf.

Baby Bear went to the whiteboard. "For each of your four main characters, I want you to write down the following information." He wrote on the board:

YOUR CHARACTER SUMMARY SHEETS
  Name:
  Role:
  Goal:
  Ambition:
  Values (two or more):
  One-sentence summary:
  One-paragraph summary:

Goldilocks took a picture of the board with her phone. "Why do you want more than one Value?"

"Because most people have several things they value. And those can be in conflict. And when a person has conflicting Values, that leads to internal conflict, and the person becomes unpredictable."

The Big Bad Wolf had a huge, sloppy grin on his face. "I don't mean to be nosy, but isn't that a mistake there at the bottom? You're asking for a one-sentence summary and a one-paragraph summary. She already did those."

Baby Bear shook his head. "She already wrote a one-sentence summary and a one-paragraph summary for the *lead* character. But the other characters all have their own personal stories. Each one of them thinks they're the hero of their personal story. That personal story isn't the same as the personal story for the hero of your novel. You must understand the personal story of each character in your novel. You need to know what drives them, what they want in life, and how they plan to get it."

"It seems like a lot of work," said Goldilocks.

"You could just go type your novel without doing any of this," said Baby Bear.

"No, I can't! I told you, I don't know where to start."

Baby Bear pointed at the whiteboard. "Now you know where to start. Today's class is over. If you give yourself one hour per character, you could have this all done in four hours and show me what you've got tomorrow."

Goldilocks sighed. It looked like she was in for a late night.

That evening after Goldilocks put the children to bed, she sat down at her computer and began typing. And the ideas started to come. She already knew Elise's story, so that was easy. And she also partly knew Dirk's story. As she typed, things seemed to magically fall into place. Monique was a little harder, but with some effort, Goldilocks came up with some reasonable ideas for her.

But Henri.

Goldilocks *really* didn't like him. He was a slimy, middle-aged man, and all he cared about was getting Elise into bed. What a horrible person! She couldn't think of much to write about him, but it didn't matter. He was the villain, and he was going to be killed anyway, so she didn't have to work hard on him.

By midnight, Goldilocks was finished. She crawled into bed feeling like a real novelist at last. Tomorrow, she'd show her work to Baby Bear, and he'd tell her she was a brilliant storyteller, and then he'd help her on the next step.

She couldn't wait.

Chapter Seven

YOUR STORY IN ONE PAGE

The next morning, Goldilocks took her laptop to the conference and arrived very early. She was the first student in Baby Bear's classroom and waited impatiently, wondering where Baby Bear was. Didn't he know that she wanted to show him her work? This was important!

Ten minutes before the workshop was due to begin, Baby Bear walked in. He was wearing a large backpack, which he barely had time to take off before Goldilocks was at the front table with her laptop.

"Look at all this that I wrote last night!"

Baby Bear scrolled through the document. "Let's see here. Your heroine ... very nice, you've got a whole page here. I see she has two Values."

"I spent a lot of time on her Values," Goldilocks said. "Nothing is more important than her daughter, Monique. And nothing is more important than having a man who loves her."

Baby Bear stared off into space. "Tell me more about this man Henri who's been courting her."

"He's awful," Goldilocks said at once. "He's got loads of money because he's a Nazi collaborator."

"It sounds like he loves Elise quite a lot."

"He just wants to get her into bed."

"That's all he wants? To get her into bed just one time?"

"No, silly. He wants to marry her."

"That sounds like love to me."

Goldilocks sighed loudly. "I *suppose*."

"And if he's got money, wouldn't he be able to help Elise care for Monique?"

"Yes, probably. So?"

"Elise has two Values," Baby Bear said. "Nothing is more important than caring for her daughter, Monique. And nothing is more important than having a man who loves her. It seems like Henri fits both of those perfectly. If Elise married him, that ought to make her very happy."

Goldilocks stared at Baby Bear, wondering how he could be so unromantic. Bears probably didn't do romance. And anyway, Baby Bear didn't look old enough to be having relationships. He was really a very young and inexperienced bear.

Baby Bear kept studying her. "Why doesn't Elise just marry Henri?"

"Because … he's awful! He's bald and fat and … he collaborates with the Nazis!"

Baby Bear scanned the document. "I don't see any Values here that say that desirable men are hairy and muscular and fight in the Resistance."

"But … those are obvious!" Goldilocks shouted. "Nobody wants a man who's bald and fat and kills innocent people. Honestly, you really don't have much sense, do—"

"There she goes, making assumptions again," said the Big Bad Wolf.

Goldilocks spun around and glared at him. "Where did you come from? And who asked your opinion?"

"You did, when you said that nobody wants bald, fat men who kill innocent people. Well, I can tell you that a bald man is less trouble to eat than a hairy one. And if he's fat, he's much more tender and juicy. And as far as killing innocent people, if you ask me, humans aren't innocent at all—the way they're ruining the planet and driving other species to extinction. So—"

"Go away!" Goldilocks shouted. "What a horrible person you are!"

"Wolf. Not person, wolf. And by the way, you look particularly scrumptious when you're angry."

"You're impossible!" Goldilocks said. "You shouldn't make jokes like that."

The Big Bad Wolf didn't say anything.

Goldilocks wondered if he might not be joking.

"Peace!" Baby Bear said, stepping between Goldilocks and the Big Bad Wolf. "Let's stay focused, shall we? My point is that Goldilocks hasn't spelled out Elise's Values fully yet. It sounds like Elise doesn't want to be loved by just any man. He needs to be young and handsome."

"Well, of course, that's obvious."

"It's obvious to Elise, but not necessarily to everybody," said Baby Bear. "That's the problem with Values—they aren't always obvious. An old woman might prefer a bald, fat man her own age who is great at conversation, rather than a young, handsome, narcissistic man who only talks to beautiful young women."

"Very well, I'll fix that Value so it's clearer," Goldilocks said grumpily.

"And furthermore, Elise apparently believes that collaborating with the Nazis is evil."

"Well, of course, that's, um …" Goldilocks sighed.

"Obvious?" said Baby Bear. "And yet millions of people collaborated with the Nazis. Apparently, resisting Nazis wasn't a Value for everybody."

"Those people had a Value that nothing is more important than staying alive," Goldilocks said. "But everybody knows that. It's … obvious."

"You keep saying that, even though it isn't." Baby Bear kept reading. "It sounds like you may have a few more Values to add to Elise's list. But the rest of the class is here, and we need to get started."

Goldilocks noticed that the room had filled with other students. She closed her laptop and looked for a seat, but almost all the seats were taken. There was only one empty chair left, in the second row, but it was next to the Big Bad Wolf. She took the chair, but made a point of scooting as far away from him as possible.

He grinned at her and licked his lips.

Baby Bear rapped his paws on the front table for attention. "Today, we'll be talking about the next step in the Snowflake Method—the one-page synopsis."

"Yuck!" Goldilocks said. "I hate synopses! I already tried to write one of those, and it was horrible. Boring. There was this old bear yesterday who was teaching how to write a synopsis. But it didn't work for me."

"Yes, well, it works for my dad," Baby Bear said.

Goldilocks's mouth fell open. "Papa Bear is your ... father?"

"That's what Mama Bear says, and she would know."

"Mama Bear is your mother?"

"I would have thought that was obvious," Baby Bear said with a huge grin. "Perhaps you'll agree with me that what's obvious to one person isn't obvious to another. But back to the tangent. Today, we'll learn to write a one-page synopsis, and you'll find that it's now very easy."

Goldilocks folded her arms across her chest. She knew writing a synopsis was boring. She had already tried it. She wondered if maybe she could play hooky for this workshop until Baby Bear returned to something more interesting.

"Some of you are thinking that synopses are boring," Baby Bear said.

A blush crept up Goldilocks's cheeks.

"And you're right. Synopses are the most boring writing you will ever do. But they're necessary if you ever want to sell a book to a traditional publisher, because they all insist on receiving a synopsis as part of your proposal. You can't get an agent without having a brilliant synopsis."

Goldilocks felt like her stomach was filled with lead. This fiction-writing business was hard work.

"Our goal today is to find a way to write a strong synopsis quickly and painlessly," said Baby Bear. "We're already most of the way there."

The Big Bad Wolf yawned noisily.

Goldilocks shot him a disgusted look.

"We've already seen how to write a one-paragraph summary of your story," said Baby Bear. "Now just take each sentence of that paragraph and expand it into a paragraph of its own. You have five sentences. Expanding each of those will give you five paragraphs, which add up to a page. That's all."

Goldilocks couldn't believe it. That sounded too simple. There had to be a catch.

"I see that most of you brought laptops," said Baby Bear. "Writing a synopsis ought to take you about an hour. I'd like you to take twenty minutes right now to write the first two paragraphs. At the end of the twenty minutes, we'll read some of them aloud. The best example will get a prize, which I'll explain a bit later."

Goldilocks desperately wanted to win that prize. She suspected it would be writing related. Perhaps an endorsement from Baby Bear. Perhaps an introduction to an excellent agent.

The Big Bad Wolf scratched his armpit. "Good luck, Blondie," he stage-whispered.

Goldilocks flipped open her laptop and began typing furiously. She didn't need luck. And she was sick to death of the Big Bad Wolf and his bad manners.

The twenty minutes passed in a flash. Goldilocks finished her second paragraph just before Baby Bear called time.

"Who wants to read their work?" Baby Bear asked.

Goldilocks flung her hand in the air.

So did every other writer in the room.

Baby Bear chose a bald, chubby, middle-aged man near the back.

The man stood up and read his two paragraphs. They were beautiful and flawless. The man was writing a literary novel set in New York, and his synopsis sang with power.

Goldilocks wanted to shrink into the floor. She could never write like that.

The Big Bad Wolf leaned toward her and whispered, "Beautiful writing, but no story. There's no there there."

"Who's next?" Baby Bear said.

Again, dozens of hands shot up.

Baby Bear chose an older woman to read. She was chubby, with frowzy hair, and Goldilocks thought her makeup seemed very poorly done. She was writing erotica, and her first two paragraphs were extremely steamy.

Goldilocks felt her cheeks burning. She couldn't believe people would write that sort of thing, much less read it in public.

The Big Bad Wolf said in a shocked whisper, "Is that even *possible* for a human?"

When Baby Bear asked for the next volunteer, Goldilocks again raised her hand, but she seemed to be invisible to Baby Bear.

After several writers had read their work, Goldilocks began getting frustrated. She didn't have a chance.

Something tapped her on the shoulder. Something warm and furry. A wolfish paw.

Goldilocks tried to ignore it.

The paw kept tapping insistently.

Finally, she turned to glare at the Big Bad Wolf.

He leaned toward her. "Want me to get Baby Bear's attention?"

Part of Goldilocks wanted to tell him to go jump off a cliff. But part of her thought that he might really be able to help. She felt so desperate, she gave a little nod.

After the next writer finished reading, Baby Bear said, "Who's next?"

The Big Bad Wolf stood up and waved both his paws. "Yo! Over here! Blondie wants to read her stuff real bad! You listening to me, Baby Bear?"

Goldilocks wanted to die. How could the Big Bad Wolf humiliate her like that?

Baby Bear smiled. "Ah, it looks like you two have made up. Very good. Please read the beginning of your synopsis, Goldilocks."

Goldilocks stood up and began reading:

"It's May of 1944, and the Allies are desperate to destroy a crucial ammunition dump before D-Day. They train half a dozen commandos to parachute behind enemy lines, armed with guns and explosives. But the plane is nearly destroyed by anti-aircraft fire, and only one commando gets out of the plane alive. Dirk Steele parachutes into France, landing in the garden of a house in a small village twenty kilometers from the target. In the darkness, he lands badly and breaks his ankle."

Goldilocks paused for breath.

The entire room had gone very quiet.

"The garden is owned by Elise Renoir, a young French widow who has an eight-year-old daughter named Monique, who has Down syndrome. Elise is terrified that the Nazis will take her away because she's 'defective.' Elise longs to fight in the Resistance. She is not afraid to die, but if she were killed, what would happen to her daughter? When she discovers Dirk unconscious in her garden, Elise knows that the safe thing would be to turn him in to the Nazis, but she can't. So she hides him in her root cellar and sets his broken ankle in a makeshift cast. For a week, Elise wrestles with her conscience. Elise has a suitor whom she hates, a bald, middle-aged collaborator named Henri. When Henri comes to court Elise and discovers Dirk, Elise kills him and buries him in her garden."

Goldilocks stopped. "That's all I have so far."

The room burst into applause.

Baby Bear was jumping up and down with excitement. "Superb! That was excellent. Your first paragraph gave us the big picture. You set the time, the place, and the stakes, which are very high. You also introduced the love interest, Dirk, and gave him a problem. Then in the second paragraph, you introduced your lead character, Elise, gave her two problems—her daughter and her unsuitable suitor—and ended with a disaster. Very soon, the villagers will be wondering what happened to Henri. Elise is committed now. Bravo!"

Goldilocks was glowing with pride. She had done it! She had written at least part of a synopsis that wasn't boring.

"I think we have a winner," said the Big Bad Wolf.

Goldilocks spun her head to look at him. "I ... thought Baby Bear was going to pick the winner."

The Big Bad Wolf produced a business card from somewhere in his mangy fur. He handed it to Goldilocks. "The prize is a one-hour appointment with me."

His card read: The Big Bad Wolf Literary Agency. It had an address in New York City.

Goldilocks was suddenly finding it hard to breathe. The Big Bad Wolf was an agent? From New York?

"Let's have lunch," said the Big Bad Wolf. "You interest me."

Baby Bear clapped his paws in delight. "Excellent! Goldilocks, you may not know it, but the Big Bad Wolf is a very good agent. He's young and hungry, and he's a tough negotiator with the editors. I suppose it's his big teeth or his sharp claws."

"It's my roguish good looks." The Big Bad Wolf ran his paws through his ragged fur.

Goldilocks shivered. What was her husband going to say when he heard that she was having lunch with such a shady character?

The Big Bad Wolf licked his lips. "Do you like pork ribs?"

"Y-yes," Goldilocks said.

"I suppose you don't like them raw."

"Um, barbecued."

His face fell. "Well, I suppose that's second best. I know a place, if you don't mind driving over to the rough side of town. It's just a little hole-in-the-wall kind of place, but the ribs are said to be excellent."

Goldilocks felt a rush of fear in her belly. This was starting to sound just a bit scary.

Baby Bear rang a little bell on his desk. "It's time for our morning break. We'll meet back here in fifteen minutes to work on step 5 in the Snowflake Method."

Chapter Eight

YOUR PEOPLE'S SECRET STORIES

*D*uring the midmorning break, Goldilocks realized that the other students were all acting strangely. As if she were somebody special. Like she knew what she was doing.

She didn't understand why they thought that. If they found out she was a fraud, they would all hate her. She was very lucky that Baby Bear was giving her so much extra help. But she also felt a bit queasy about the Big Bad Wolf's sudden interest in her. What if it wasn't her writing that he liked? What if it was … something else? Goldilocks shivered. Surely, Baby Bear wouldn't have invited him to this conference if he were a wicked person?

When the students returned to the room, Goldilocks saw that Little Pig had a very satisfied expression on his face.

The Big Bad Wolf was nowhere in sight.

Baby Bear glared at Little Pig. "The Big Bad Wolf has paid his debt to society. There was no reason for you to tell the conference director about his … past."

Little Pig snorted. "If it were a couple of *bears* he had brutally murdered, you wouldn't feel safe with him walking around. You heard him boasting about eating pigs. What were you thinking, to invite him to this conference when you knew I'd be here?"

Goldilocks felt cold all over. The Big Bad Wolf? A murderer?

Baby Bear folded his paws across his chest. "I'm quite convinced that he's reformed his ways. He's a well-respected literary agent now, and he is no danger at all to anybody at this conference."

Little Pig smirked. "We'll just see if the conference director agrees."

"If she does, then I'll give her a piece of my mind." Baby Bear savagely flung open his laptop. "Now we've wasted enough time on this foolishness. On to the next step in the Snowflake."

A low murmur ran around the room.

Goldilocks wondered if she should ditch her lunch appointment with the Big Bad Wolf.

"You've all written the first two paragraphs in your one-page synopsis, and it was easy, wasn't it?" Baby Bear said. "Not as boring as you might have thought—because you're focusing on the disasters. Your homework tonight will be to finish your synopsis. But in the meantime, we're going to work on your characters next."

Mrs. Hubbard said, "I thought we already did that yesterday?"

"In the Snowflake Method, we alternate. We work on your plot, then your characters, then your plot, then your characters, each time going deeper. Yesterday, when we did the third step of the Snowflake, it was fairly superficial character work. Names, Goals, Ambitions, Values—that sort of thing. Today, we're going to get inside the skin of your characters."

Baby Bear paused to take a drink of water from a bottle of Evian on his table.

Goldilocks opened her laptop to take notes. She could hardly wait for this next step. She loved character-oriented fiction. Her favorite authors dove deep inside the psyches of their characters. Baby Bear probably had very little to teach her on this subject, but she might pick up a tidbit or two. And she might surprise him with her stunning knowledge of the subject.

"Who wants to be on the hot seat?" Baby Bear asked.

Goldilocks didn't say anything. She would love to get more help on her characters, but she didn't want to hog attention.

Little Pig raised his right front hoof. "I don't need any help on my characters, because they're based on real-life people— including a very high-ranking executive pig. But I'd like to hire somebody to help me with my manuscript, and I'm paying top dollar." He shot a look at Goldilocks.

Baby Bear's face went very tight. "If ... *anybody* is interested in working with Little Pig, please meet him after class. Right now, I'd like to focus on developing *fictional* characters. Who wants to volunteer?"

Mrs. Hubbard said, "I'm dying to hear more about that story Goldilocks is writing. It sounds wonderful."

A rustle of yeses ran around the room.

"Goldilocks, it sounds like you're elected. Come on up to the hot seat," Baby Bear said.

Goldilocks felt a little faint, but she went forward and sat down. She wondered if her hair looked all right.

"Tell me about this hero in your story, Dirk Steele," said Baby Bear. "He's doing a very brave thing, parachuting into Nazi territory to blow up a place that is sure to be heavily guarded. Why is he doing that?"

"I ..." Goldilocks didn't want to say she didn't know. She hadn't really worried much about Dirk's motivation. "Well, he hates the Nazis."

"In 1944, all Americans hated the Nazis," Baby Bear said. "But Dirk is the only one I see parachuting into a French village in the dark of night with a duffel bag filled with explosives. He'll probably be killed on this mission. Why did he volunteer for such a dangerous assignment?"

Goldilocks just started talking without even thinking. She spent ten minutes explaining how Dirk grew up in a very rough neighborhood in the Bronx. He was small when he was younger, and the bigger boys often bullied him. He learned to be tough and fight back. Now that he was a grown man, big and strong, he wasn't afraid of anybody.

Dirk's best friend was a Jewish boy named Benny. Benny's uncle lived in Berlin, and his shop had been destroyed by the Nazis on Kristallnacht. Benny didn't know if his uncle was alive or dead. Dirk had volunteered for this mission because he knew there were millions of people like Benny's uncle in Europe. And he wanted to do his part to beat the Nazi bullies. Dirk wasn't afraid of anybody.

Baby Bear asked about Dirk's family.

Goldilocks explained that he had several brothers, but he wasn't married.

"What about a girlfriend?" Baby Bear said. "A big, handsome boy like Dirk should have a girlfriend, right?"

Goldilocks hadn't thought about that, so she made up something. "Well ... he did, but they broke up a month before the mission because Dirk, um, got in a bar fight with some sailors, and one of them was the brother of his girlfriend."

Baby Bear shook his head. "Dirk's training for an important mission, and he gets in a bar fight a month before? He's not too bright, is he?"

"He's very loyal!" Goldilocks said. "The sailors were picking on his friend Benny, and so Dirk put them all in the hospital."

Baby Bear said, "Dirk seems to have a protector mentality."

"Yes, he's very protective."

"But he's going to break his ankle when he lands. Then a woman will be taking care of him, protecting him. How does he feel about that?"

Goldilocks spent a few seconds thinking and then made up something about Dirk's mental conflicts, and how he would start chafing after a few days of being cooped up in the root cellar. "And ... that's why he's up in the sitting room when Henri comes to court Elise!"

"Ah, very good!" Baby Bear said.

Goldilocks sat back in her chair, thinking she had handled that extremely well. This Snowflake Method was forcing her to think about things she hadn't really worked out yet, but she could see that it was filling in the gaps in her story nicely. Every time Baby Bear asked a question, she could easily make up something on the spot to answer it. She felt very pleased that she was such a talented writer.

"So tell me about Henri," Baby Bear said.

Goldilocks shrugged. "There's not much to say. He's the villain. He's courting Elise, and he's been threatening to tell the Nazis about her daughter if she doesn't, um, ... you know." She wasn't sure if Baby Bear was old enough to know about men and women sleeping together. He was obviously a very naive young bear.

"Henri sounds like a bad man," said Baby Bear.

"Can we talk about Elise and Monique?" Goldilocks said. "I think we've done enough on Henri. I told you, he's not important."

"But he's the villain of the story, at least early on," said Baby Bear.

Goldilocks shook her head. "Villains aren't important. I don't like Henri, and I think it's a waste of time to talk about him. And anyway, he's going to be killed at the end of the first act."

"Villains are very important," Baby Bear said. "My dad published a famous story years ago, and he focused heavily on the villain. It's based on a true incident. Back when I was a cub, a human child broke into our house. She stole some of our porridge, broke our furniture, and was actually sleeping in my bed when we got home. Then she resisted arrest and escaped. Obviously an awful, wicked human, but it was a powerful story because of that."

Goldilocks felt so hot she began fanning her cheeks. "That ... sounds terrible. But perhaps if you knew the girl's background, you might understand her better. Perhaps she had a horrible childhood. Perhaps she was lost. Or hungry. Or frightened of bears. There could be … all sorts of reasons she did what she did."

Baby Bear scowled. "Hmmph! She should have gone to jail."

Goldilocks was blushing fiercely, and she desperately wanted to run away, but that would look very guilty. She couldn't bear for the other students to guess what sort of person she really was. "I don't think Papa Bear's book did a very good job with his villain. Papa Bear ought to have thought more about the girl's motivations, don't you think?"

"Yes, well … I'm sure he could have," Baby Bear said curtly. "But at least Papa Bear didn't kill off his villain right at the beginning of the story. If you're going to go easy on a real-life villain, then shouldn't you be willing to put more work into your own fictional villain?"

"Yes, of course, that's just what I was thinking, that's exactly what I was about to say." Goldilocks realized she was gabbling.

"Very well, then, I want you to treat your villain with the same respect you treat your hero," Baby Bear said. "Let's firm up your story. Right now, your story is weak."

"Weak?" Goldilocks felt her heart stutter. That wasn't true, was it? Everyone had been telling her she had an excellent story. "Whatever do you mean?"

"The strength of your story is set by the strength of your villain," Baby Bear said. "Strong villain, strong story. Weak villain, weak story. And you have a very weak villain."

"The Nazis are my villain," Goldilocks said.

"Nonsense. The Nazis are abstract. I can't visualize a million Nazis. I can visualize one bald, fat French collaborator who wants to get your heroine in bed. But right now, he's weak and boring. You've made him unattractive, and he's so stupid that he gets himself killed in the first act."

Goldilocks didn't know what to think. "You said that was good."

"It was good for your heroine. It forced her to commit to the story. But it was bad for your story tension, because it got rid of your villain."

"Why didn't you say something if it was so awful?"

Baby Bear smiled. "Because it isn't *awful*. There are things to like in your story. But you have a weak villain. And now it's time to make him stronger."

"But ... how? What do I have to do?"

"I want you to put yourself inside the skin of Henri," Baby Bear said. "Figure out what makes him tick. Everybody has a secret story that nobody else knows. I want to know Henri's secret story. I want to understand why he does what he does. So tell us Henri's secret story—the story in which he's the hero. And when you've done that, we can go back and rework your earlier steps."

"But we've put so much work into my story!" Goldilocks said.

Baby Bear looked exasperated. "Close your eyes and imagine that you're Henri. In 1944, you are middle-aged. Therefore, you were born around 1900 in a small village in France. Tell me your secret story."

"Well ..." Goldilocks felt her mind racing. "I was short and chubby as a child, and the other children picked on me. As I got older, I never got big and strong like Dirk, so I had to use my brains. I learned to pit my enemies against each other."

"Give me an example of how you did that," said Baby Bear.

"In high school, there were two handsome and popular boys who often picked on me," Goldilocks said. "Charles and Michel. So I sent Charles a love letter that was purportedly from Michel's girlfriend. Charles thought it was real and tried to seduce the girl. Michel found out and they had a huge fight. Michel lost an eye, and Charles was forced to leave town and join the army."

"Did you fight in World War I?" Baby Bear asked.

"I enlisted as soon as I was old enough, but I had poor eyesight and couldn't shoot, so I worked as a cook. I always felt ashamed that I couldn't fight for my country."

"What happened after the war?" asked Baby Bear. "Things were very bad, weren't they?"

Goldilocks nodded. "Yes, there was the Spanish flu. Then terrible economic times. I found work keeping the books for a criminal organization."

Goldilocks spun out a long story about Henri scratching out a living in postwar France, marrying a homely woman because he had got her pregnant, then living through the Great Depression and losing both his child and wife in an auto accident. And making many enemies of the honest people in the town, who hated the gangster that Henri worked for.

"Then the Nazis came, and I saw that there was no way to fight them. The Resistance was disorganized and foolhardy. I had to do what the Nazis said, or they would kill me. Everybody in town hated me, but there was one person who never treated me with contempt."

"Who was that?" Baby Bear asked.

"The little girl, Monique. Elise's child."

"What did Monique do that made you feel special?" Baby Bear asked.

"She brought me flowers every morning and left them on my doorstep." Goldilocks still had her eyes closed, and she could picture little Monique creeping to Henri's door every morning very early and leaving an armful of roses. "And she smiled at me. Nobody else smiled at me. I thought that her mother, Elise, must be a very kind woman, to have such a daughter."

"Would you ever hurt little Monique?" Baby Bear asked. "Would you ever turn her in to the Nazis?"

"I'd … rather die first." Goldilocks shuddered and opened her eyes. She found that she was crying. For a few moments, she had felt like she really was Henri. It was a very disconcerting feeling, because Henri was the villain. She had thought she hated him. But now she also felt a little love in her heart for him. She loved him and hated him, both at the same time. She knew that didn't make sense, but it was just how she felt.

Baby Bear was looking at his watch. "It's almost noon. Are there any final comments before we break for lunch?"

Little Pig snorted loudly. "I think you've ruined your villain, Goldilocks. Now he's a sappy, stupid, sentimental person. But don't take my word for it. You're having lunch with the Big Bad Wolf, and he's going to laugh in your face and tell you that Henri is the worst villain in the history of fiction."

The lunch bell rang.

All the students stood up and hurried out.

Goldilocks sat on the chair with her eyes closed, hoping to ask Baby Bear's opinion when everybody was gone.

But when the hubbub died down and she opened her eyes, the room was empty.

And now she had to face the Big Bad Wolf and tell him about her sappy, stupid, sentimental villain. This was going to be the worst day of her life.

Chapter Nine

YOUR SECOND DISASTER AND YOUR MORAL PREMISE

oldilocks headed toward the cafeteria, hoping to find a quiet spot in a corner where she could eat lunch without the Big Bad Wolf seeing her.

But just as she reached the cafeteria door, she felt a tap on her shoulder.

"Oh, my!" She spun around.

The Big Bad Wolf was grinning at her. "I've been looking all over for you, Blondie. Let's go to lunch. I'm famished."

"L-lunch?" Goldilocks wanted to say that she'd really rather eat in the cafeteria. That she didn't want to go anywhere with a convicted murderer. But somehow, she just couldn't get the words out.

"At Barbie's Barbecue House," said the Big Bad Wolf. "Did you forget? We've got reservations in fifteen minutes, so we need to hurry."

"O-okay." Goldilocks meekly followed the Big Bad Wolf through the lunch crowd and up the walk and past the coffee shop and into the parking lot and all the way to his car. Her stomach churned with fear, but she got in. The car was a long, shiny black Lincoln rental with a leather interior and powerful air-conditioning.

The Big Bad Wolf handed Goldilocks his phone and asked her to navigate.

She felt cold sweat spring up all over her body. She was really doing this. She was driving away from the conference with a complete stranger, a convicted murderer. A wolf who talked casually about eating people.

And why? Just because he was a big-shot literary agent? Because she was too polite to back out? Because she couldn't say no? Why couldn't she learn to be a little more assertive?

Goldilocks discreetly felt inside her purse and fingered her pepper spray. She had taken a training course only a few weeks ago. If he tried anything, she'd spray him right in the eyes and then scream for help.

The Big Bad Wolf spent the entire drive complaining about an editor who had called him during the break to renegotiate a non-compete clause for an author who was working with two different publishers and doing some indie work on the side. He sounded very angry and bared his teeth when he said that some editors weren't good for anything except a three-hour lunch.

Goldilocks felt more and more frightened as they drove. She could see that Little Pig was right. The Big Bad Wolf was tough and brash and quite possibly dangerous. He was going to ask about her characters, and she was going to have to tell him that she had turned Henri into a wimp.

Could she change Henri back into a one-dimensional villain?

No, she could not. Baby Bear had been right. Great villains needed to be three-dimensional. She had made Henri three-dimensional, and she was not going to change him back.

Could she bend the truth and tell the Big Bad Wolf what he wanted to hear?

No, never. The Big Bad Wolf would be furious if he took her on as a client and then found out she'd lied to him.

He wasn't going to like her villain, and she was just going to have to tell him. For once in her life, Goldilocks was going to have to stand up for herself. She liked who her villain was becoming, and if the Big Bad Wolf didn't like it, then he was the wrong agent for her.

"There's the place." Goldilocks pointed at the barbecue house. It looked magnificent. "You said it was a little hole in the wall."

The Big Bad Wolf grinned and showed all his teeth. "Didn't want you to be disappointed. It's getting great reviews, so I expect it's fantastic. And lunch is on me, of course—business expense."

Goldilocks wasn't sure what to say, so she said, "Thank you." But she knew the wolf would hate her when he found out that he had bought lunch for a very unsuitable client.

ive minutes later, they were inside the restaurant. The Big Bad Wolf ordered pork ribs. "As rare as possible," he told the waiter.

"And I'll have mine well done," Goldilocks said.

The waiter disappeared, and the Big Bad Wolf studied Goldilocks intently. "Baby Bear texted me that the class helped you work on your characters before lunch. Bring me up to speed. I like your story, but characters sell a book to an editor."

Goldilocks felt her heart hammering. "I don't know where to begin."

"Start with your heroine."

"We didn't really talk much about Elise—"

"Good, no point in that. You've probably spent ten years thinking about Elise. I bet she's a lot like you, and you know her inside out."

Goldilocks nodded. "So we spent some time talking about my hero, Dirk Steele."

The Big Bad Wolf nodded. "What's he most afraid of?"

"He's not afraid of anything."

"Everybody's afraid of something."

"What are you afraid of?"

He looked shocked for a moment, and a haunted look came into his eyes. Then he shook his head and gave her a wolfish grin. "Nice try, but let's stick to your novel. I want to hear about Dirk. What's he afraid of?"

Goldilocks spent a few minutes spinning out a tale of how Dirk had been bitten by a rat when he was very young, and so now he was afraid of rats.

The Big Bad Wolf didn't say much.

Goldilocks thought he looked rather disappointed, but reading a wolf's expression was much harder than reading a human's.

The waiter came with their food, and they both dug in.

The Big Bad Wolf turned out to have excellent manners. Goldilocks had wondered if maybe he'd eat like a dog, gnawing at his food and chomping noisily, but he ate with the polished precision of a Boston blueblood. He asked Goldilocks what her personal vision was.

"I just … want to be a best-selling novelist. I want people to know my name."

The Big Bad Wolf was nodding. "Sounds like the theme song from *Fame*."

Goldilocks felt her cheeks burning. "I suppose that's very shallow of me."

"No, no, not at all," said the Big Bad Wolf. "The big drivers for most people are power, money, sex, or fame. Personally, fame is what drives me. Ten years from now, I want people to hear my name and think, 'The world's best literary agent.'"

"You'll get there," Goldilocks said. "What could possibly stop you?"

The Big Bad Wolf looked so desperately sad for a moment that Goldilocks wanted to cry. "Is something wrong?" she asked.

He shook his head fiercely. "We're getting off track. Tell me about your villain. This Henri person. What makes him tick?"

Goldilocks felt just a little dizzy. The Big Bad Wolf wasn't going to like what she had to say. She reminded herself that it was his problem, and then began talking about Henri. His difficult childhood. His harassment by school bullies. His disappointment at not being a real soldier during the Great War. His wife and child. His emptiness after they died. His shame at collaborating with the Nazis, and his loneliness when the villagers shunned him. And how much he loved Elise's daughter, Monique, the only person who treated him as if he were a real person.

She spent the whole time looking at her food, afraid to meet the Big Bad Wolf's eyes.

When she finished, there was dead silence.

Goldilocks looked at the Big Bad Wolf.

He was scowling.

"Is something wrong?" Goldilocks couldn't seem to catch her breath. Little Pig had been right. He hated it.

"This is going to completely change your story," said the Big Bad Wolf. "You do understand that, don't you?"

Goldilocks felt her heart double-thump. "If you don't like it, I'm sorry I wasted your time. But my heart tells me this is the right direction, and I'm not going to …" She sucked in her breath. "I'm not going to change it."

The Big Bad Wolf narrowed his eyes.

Goldilocks wanted to die. "Can I just explain why, before you reject me? Baby Bear made me put myself in Henri's shoes. So I asked myself how he could look in the mirror every morning and not shoot himself. And I realized that everybody, even the worst villain, sees themselves as the hero of their story. And once I did that, I saw that there was more to Henri than just a wicked villain. Baby Bear was right, and I was wrong. So don't try to change my mind. And I'll … I'll pay for my own lunch."

Tears began streaming out of the Big Bad Wolf's eyes.

Goldilocks was so astonished she didn't know what to think.

"I love what you've done with Henri." The Big Bad Wolf

smeared the back of his paw across his eyes. "You can't imagine what it's like being the villain of a story and having everyone hate you."

Goldilocks could imagine. She was very lucky that Papa Bear didn't know the identity of the anonymous little girl in his novel. She put her hand on the Big Bad Wolf's paw and patted it gently. "I ... guess I don't follow the news," Goldilocks said. "But it sounds like you were once accused of ... murder?"

"Double murder," said the Big Bad Wolf. "Years ago. I didn't do it, but try telling anybody that. My uncle had been a notorious murderer. You must have heard about Little Red's grandmother?"

"Oh, my!" Goldilocks had grown up hearing about Little Red and the wolf who ate her grandmother. All over Goldilocks's body, her skin felt cold. She couldn't think what to say.

"Ten years ago, I was accused of murdering two little pigs," said the Big Bad Wolf. "I was asleep when it happened, at home in my bed. Somehow, I slept for twenty-four hours straight, which is totally out of character for me. But I couldn't prove it, and there were wolf tracks at the murder scene that matched me perfectly. I was convicted on circumstantial evidence and sent to prison."

Goldilocks remembered vaguely hearing something about that. She had been in college, and the murder of two little pigs by some evil wolf had seemed far away and unimportant.

The Big Bad Wolf looked at her with huge, mournful eyes.

Goldilocks wanted to cry. "And now you can't ever live that down."

He shook his head. "No, I can't. I was framed and I came from a bad family, with an infamous uncle who had my exact same name. The jury came in believing I was guilty. I had a lousy public defender and no alibi, and I never had a chance."

Goldilocks believed him. She couldn't quite say why, but she felt absolutely certain that he'd been framed.

"Baby Bear thinks I've reformed," said the Big Bad Wolf. "But he's wrong. I was never a murderer in the first place."

"I believe you," said Goldilocks. "You talk rough and you say frightening things, but I think it's just an act. I think you're really a very kind and gentle wolf."

The Big Bad Wolf growled and showed his teeth. "Don't you dare tell a soul, or the editors will stop being afraid of me."

Goldilocks laughed.

"So. Back to your novel," said the Big Bad Wolf. "You've completely changed your villain. That's going to have major repercussions."

"Little Pig says I've ruined my story," Goldilocks said.

The Big Bad Wolf snorted. "Nonsense. Ignore that bacon-brained idiot. He doesn't know anything about fiction. You've changed your story, and it's going to be a lot better. But now you need to rethink everything."

"So ... you're still interested in me?" Goldilocks couldn't believe it. "You looked angry when I told you what I'd come up with for Henri."

The Big Bad Wolf grinned and leaned forward. "Hope I didn't scare you, but I had to see what you were made of. I like a writer who can stand up for herself, be true to her story."

"R-really?" Goldilocks stared at him. "But I thought you liked ... you know, strong villains."

"Oh, I do, I do," the Big Bad Wolf said. "And Henri is turning out a lot stronger than I expected. The way you were talking yesterday, he was this seedy little two-dimensional, boring villain who is bad just because he likes to be bad."

"But you didn't say anything yesterday."

"That's why I invited you to lunch. To discuss the problems I was seeing. But it looks like you've got your story back on track. So tell me about Henri's Values."

"Nothing is more important than life. And nothing is more important than honor."

"Honor?" said the Big Bad Wolf. "Talk to me about honor. That's a very big Value among wolves. In fact, for a wolf, absolutely nothing is more important than honor. It's our preeminent cultural Value. Not so much among humans."

"Well, if you ever read *The Godfather*, you'd know that some humans have honor as their highest Value," said Goldilocks.

Surprise slashed across the Big Bad Wolf's face. "You've read *The Godfather*?"

"It's ... one of my favorite books." Goldilocks blushed. "I suppose that makes me a bad person."

"It's one of my favorite books too." The Big Bad Wolf leaned forward, and he studied Goldilocks intently. "What do you like about *The Godfather*?"

"I always thought it was just amazing how Mario Puzo created a compelling character who's so evil, and yet thinks he's so good. And he *is* good in a twisted kind of way. He helps poor widows without asking for payment. He rights wrongs done to his people. He protects the sons of his community from being drafted. As long as they pay him honor. That's the whole basis of his wealth—his honor. Without honor, he'd be nothing."

"Which is what drives the story, when his oldest son shows him dishonor," said the Big Bad Wolf. "How does honor drive Henri in your story?"

"He's been dishonored all his life. As a child. In school. In the army. After the Great War, the townspeople spit in his path because he worked for a criminal. And then the Nazis took over France, and he collaborated with them out of fear, but they didn't respect him, because he was a traitor. Henri has spent his whole life being dissed by everybody for being a wimp, and he thinks he's more than that."

"And so what is his Ambition?"

"He wants to be respected. He wants to be a man of honor."

"Good, that's abstract," said the Big Bad Wolf. "It makes a good Ambition. How can you turn that into a concrete Goal? What would it look like for him to be a man of honor?"

"What he desperately wants is to do something great. Something noble. Something that means something. Something that will atone for his past life of collaboration."

"That's all abstract. What could he do, after a lifetime of being a weasel?"

Goldilocks felt her heart thumping. "He could blow up the ammo dump. When Dirk and Elise fail, he could blow it up himself."

"Whoa, whoa, whoa!" said the Big Bad Wolf. "I thought you killed Henri at the end of Act 1. What's he doing still alive at the end of your story?"

"Oh, well, I was going to tell you that," said Goldilocks. "I can't kill him at the end of Act 1."

"Give me your new one-paragraph summary, and I want three good, solid, screaming disasters."

Goldilocks took out her laptop. "Actually, this is all so new that I haven't written any of it down. Can I type it out as I talk?"

The Big Bad Wolf nodded. "Whatever works for you."

Goldilocks opened her one-paragraph summary document, made a copy, and then retyped it as she talked.

"Elise Renoir is a young widow in Nazi-occupied France, and Dirk Steele is an American saboteur who parachutes into her backyard and breaks his leg, three weeks before D-Day. Elise cares for Dirk for a week, but then her unwanted suitor Henri discovers them, and threatens to turn in Dirk to the authorities unless Elise agrees to marry him. Elise sends her daughter Monique away to a remote village for a few weeks, planning to join her after helping Dirk blow up his target, but Monique is captured by the Nazis, who intend to send her to a death camp. Elise joins forces with the Resistance and persuades Henri to help her and Dirk ambush Monique's transport truck, but in the fighting, Dirk is fatally wounded. Dirk and Elise take the truck to the ammo dump, evading Nazis all the way, and blow it up the day before the Allied invasion begins."

The Big Bad Wolf was smiling. "I like it. This is a stronger story. In this version, you've got Elise joining the Resistance. What happened there? She was afraid to do that before."

"She realized that living in fear just leads to disaster, so she decided to try living in courage and see if that leads to victory."

"Yes!" shouted the Big Bad Wolf. He jumped out of his chair and began dancing around, raising his arms in the air. "Touchdown!"

The other diners were staring at him and Goldilocks.

She decided she didn't care. Something had just happened. She wasn't quite sure what, but it sounded like she'd made a breakthrough.

The Big Bad Wolf sat down. "I think you've just found the Moral Premise for your story."

"The *what?*" Goldilocks said, feeling slightly offended. "I'm not trying to write some cheap little morality tale."

"Of course not," said the Big Bad Wolf. "But every good story has a Moral Premise. You can read all about it in the book *The Moral Premise* by Stan Williams. The basic idea is that in the first half of the story, the lead character lives by a false Moral Premise, and reaps the results."

"So Elise's false Moral Premise is …?"

"That she has to live in fear to be safe," said the Big Bad Wolf.

"But living in fear leads to disaster."

The Big Bad Wolf nodded. "And as a result of the second disaster—right at the midpoint of the story—the lead character changes to a true Moral Premise. She decides that she can live by courage."

"Which leads to victory."

"Yes. Not necessarily a victory in the outer sense," said the Big Bad Wolf. "Elise may fail to get back her daughter. She may fail to blow up the ammo dump. She may even fail to survive. But the important thing is that she is a victor in her soul. Virtue is its own reward."

Goldilocks thought it was very odd to be hearing about virtue from a wolf who was a convicted murderer.

The Big Bad Wolf was smiling. "This is so much fun. There's nothing I like more than helping a writer find her story." He looked at his watch. "Unfortunately, we need to get back to the conference. But let me be clear—I love where your story is going. You've made some dramatic progress today."

"And now I've got a lot of work ahead of me," said Goldilocks.

After she fixed her villain, her story had changed radically.

Which meant she now had to rethink everything.

She was going to give Baby Bear an earful about this.

If his Snowflake Method was so good, then why did she have to make all these changes to her story?

Chapter Ten

WHY BACKTRACKING IS GOOD

*G*oldilocks marched into the classroom exactly on time. The Big Bad Wolf ambled in after her. There weren't many seats left, but Goldilocks found one midway back. The Big Bad Wolf took one in the very back row.

Baby Bear stood in front, grinning at both of them. "Do I dare ask how lunch went?"

"The ribs were great," said the Big Bad Wolf. "Pork ribs. Big and juicy and as rare as the chef could—"

"Make him stop!" shouted Little Pig. "Wolf, you just watch yourself, or you'll be going back to the penitentiary!"

The Big Bad Wolf showed his teeth and growled fiercely. "Might I invite you to dinner this evening? If you bring some fava beans and a nice Chianti—"

"Enough, both of you!" said Baby Bear. "Goldilocks, did you have a productive meeting with the Big Bad Wolf? You seemed a little unsure whether those changes to your villain were going to work out."

"My villain's *fine*," Goldilocks said in her huffiest voice.

"Yup, brilliantissimo," said the Big Bad Wolf. "I'm already thinking of editors I know who are going to love her story."

Baby Bear's eyes shunted from Goldilocks to the Big Bad Wolf and then back again. "Is something wrong, Goldilocks? It sounds like you've got a pretty strong vote of confidence from the Big Bad Wolf."

"I told you, I'm *fine*." Goldilocks crossed her arms on her chest and scowled at him.

"You don't look fine. You look upset about something."

Goldilocks could not believe he was being so obtuse. "You promised to teach us how to Snowflake our novels."

Baby Bear just looked at her. "That's exactly what I've been doing. You've now made it through the first five steps, and you're doing great."

"Spectacular," said the Big Bad Wolf. "Super. Mondo. Groovy."

"I am *not* doing great," said Goldilocks. "Just before lunch, in case you didn't notice, I made some huge changes to my villain, and now my *whole story* needs fixing. How is that great? I'm going to have to redo *everything*."

Baby Bear shrugged. "I suppose that might seem like a problem. But it's a good problem, and I was just going to teach on why backtracking is essential. Let's take a little inventory, shall we? You've completed five steps of the Snowflake Method. How long will it take you to change step 1, which was your one-sentence summary?"

Goldilocks flipped open her laptop. "Um, actually, that one won't need any changing. It's … fine as it is."

Baby Bear nodded. "That's what I thought, but just wanted to check. I recommend that my students constantly try to improve their one-sentence summary. What about step 2, your one-paragraph summary? Obviously, that was going to need some changing after you reworked your villain. How long will that take to fix up?"

"She did that at lunch," said the Big Bad Wolf. "You people ought to hear it now. It's awesomely better. Goldilocks redid it in about five minutes while we were talking. Man, this story really zings. Looks like we might have a shot at redemption for this villain."

"Redemption—pffffft!" said Little Pig. "Once a villain, always a villain."

Mrs. Hubbard shook a long, bony finger at Little Pig. "Nonsense, young pig! People can change. Even wolves can change. But what never changes is when you've got an empty cupboard."

Baby Bear was rocking back and forth on his heels. "It sounds like Goldilocks is upset about having to rework this step of the Snowflake. She spent five minutes revising her one-paragraph summary." He went to the whiteboard and wrote down, FIVE MINUTES.

Little Pig bunched his long pink snout into a sneer. "But her character sheets in step 3 are a lost cause. She spent hours on those last night, and now all that effort is a sunk cost."

Goldilocks opened the document with her character sheets and scanned down the page. "Um, I guess they're not *all* wrong. The one for Elise won't change at all, except I need to rewrite the one-paragraph summary for her personal story. But it's the same as the one-paragraph summary for the novel, so I'll just need to paste that in."

"And then there's Dirk," said the Big Bad Wolf. "I imagine that'll take you days and weeks to change."

Goldilocks looked at her character sheet for Dirk. Nothing really needed changing except his one-paragraph summary, and she could see that it was going to be very similar to the changes she'd made for Elise. "I think it'll only take me a few minutes to change that one."

"Oh, well, there's Monique!" said the Big Bad Wolf. "Hours and days to change that!"

Goldilocks shook her head. "No, it'll take only a few minutes for her. The real problem is going to be Henri's one-paragraph summary. That's going to change like crazy."

Baby Bear shrugged. "I suppose that happens sometimes. Read us what you had already written for Henri."

Goldilocks scrolled down.

The entry for Henri was completely blank.

Her face suddenly felt very hot. "Oh, my!"

The Big Bad Wolf came over to look at her screen. He sat back on his haunches and began howling with laughter. He laughed so hard, he fell over and lay on the floor, clutching his stomach and shaking.

Goldilocks wanted to die of embarrassment. "Actually, it looks like I didn't do anything on step 3 for Henri, other than write his name."

Baby Bear nodded. "I thought I remembered his part being a little thin. I seem to recall that you didn't like him much, because he was such a mean, nasty, evil, wicked—"

"Don't say things like that about Henri!" Goldilocks shouted. "He had a terrible childhood, and there are reasons he turned out the way he did."

"—gangster-serving, selfish, greedy, grasping, woman-chasing, pigheaded—"

"You say that like it's a bad thing," said Little Pig.

"—rascally, Nazi-collaborating scoundrel," said Baby Bear. "So you didn't bother to write anything about him, because he's just a villain."

Goldilocks hung her head. "Well, I was wrong, so I suppose I need to backtrack and write up something for him in step 3."

"I suppose you do," said Baby Bear. "How much time extra is that going to cost you?"

"Well … not any extra time, because I never did it in the first place," Goldilocks said. "But if your Snowflake Method was any good, it would have forced me to do it before I moved on. Now I have to backtrack."

"There's nothing wrong with backtracking," Baby Bear said.

"It's essential, in fact. All writers backtrack. It's just a matter of how *much* they have to backtrack."

The Big Bad Wolf had finished laughing. He got up and returned to his seat. "You want to hear a horror story?" he said. "I had an author last year who got his revision letter from his editor, and it basically had only two words: 'Start over.'"

"Ouch! Start *over*?" Baby Bear shook his head sadly.

"What's a revision letter?" asked Goldilocks.

"After you sell your novel, you'll spend some time polishing it until it's as perfect as you can make it," Baby Bear said. "Then you send it to your publisher. They assign it to an editor, who reads it carefully, makes notes, and writes a revision letter telling you what's working well in the story and what's broken. The letter doesn't tell you how to fix it. That's not the editor's job. She's there to point out the major problems. Your job, after you get the revision letter, is to rewrite your manuscript."

"Actually, the author's job is more complicated than that," said the Big Bad Wolf. "When an author gets a revision letter, she's required by law to call her agent and complain bitterly about her mean, nasty, cruel editor who has bacon for brains. She whines and moans and complains for three hours. If she's the emotional sort, she cries big buckets of tears. If she's the unemotional sort, she makes secret plans to send her editor a letter bomb. Then her wise and brilliant agent talks her off the ledge, reminds her that she signed a binding legal contract, and suggests that maybe her editor might have said one or two non-moronic things in the revision letter."

"And eventually, when the author's sanity returns, she rewrites her manuscript," said Baby Bear.

"So, what's your point?" said Goldilocks. "What does this have to do with backtracking?"

"Rewriting your manuscript *is* backtracking," said Baby Bear. "Rewriting it all completely from scratch is the worst form of backtracking."

"I only see that with my seat-of-the-pants writers," said the Big Bad Wolf. "Yeah, sure, *sometimes* they nail their first draft, but sometimes, hoo-boy, they turn in the most wretched drivel you ever heard of. And they always think it's brilliant."

"The point here," said Baby Bear, "is that when you have to backtrack on a full manuscript, you're looking at six months of hard labor."

"And the publisher gives you one month to do it," said the Big Bad Wolf. "Loads of fun!"

"You said all writers have to backtrack," said Goldilocks. "Does that mean outliners and Snowflakers do too?"

"Of course," said Baby Bear. "When an outliner backtracks, he has to revise his outline. If that's a hundred pages, he does a hundred pages of revision. That's better than rewriting a four-hundred-page manuscript, but it's still a lot of work."

"But ... Snowflakers have to backtrack too?" Goldilocks said, determined to make Baby Bear admit the point.

"Of course!" said Baby Bear. "That's what I've been trying to tell you. Everybody backtracks. You'll never get it perfect on the first round. During the ten steps of the Snowflake, I encourage writers to backtrack after every single step if they need to."

"That sounds dreadful!" Goldilocks cried.

"Not if it's only five or ten minutes of work," said the Big Bad Wolf. "Which is what you're looking at here, Blondie. And since you didn't do the work in the first place, technically, it isn't even backtracking. You're just doing the steps out of order."

"Oh," Goldilocks said in a very small voice.

"Backtracking is *good*," said Baby Bear. "It makes your story stronger, deeper, richer. The reason Snowflakers love the Snowflake Method is because they do a lot of their backtracking early, on small pieces of work. Which means that they don't have to do much backtracking later, when it's ballooned out to a four-hundred-page manuscript. It's a lot easier to revise a one-page synopsis than a whole novel."

Goldilocks opened up her one-page synopsis to see how much she had to change. She had only written the first two paragraphs of that synopsis, and it turned out she only needed to change the last sentence of the second paragraph—the sentence where Elise killed Henri and buried him in the garden.

"So, Goldilocks," Baby Bear said. "Can you give us an estimate of how much time it's going to cost you to backtrack?"

Goldilocks didn't say anything.

"Hours?" said the Big Bad Wolf. "Days? Weeks?"

"About … ten minutes," Goldilocks said.

Baby Bear smiled. "Well, then."

"No way!" said the young man next to Goldilocks. "I didn't sign up to learn how to keep chewing over the same piece of gum a thousand times. I'm out of here." He grabbed his backpack and shambled out of the room.

Baby Bear's mouth dropped open. "Is there anyone else who thinks this is too hard and wants to leave?"

Goldilocks thought it was horribly rude to walk out in the middle of a workshop.

But one by one, half a dozen other writers quietly grabbed their things and walked out.

Little Pig raised his hoof. "Can we get on with it? The reason people are abandoning you is because you're telling us things we don't want to hear. Nobody wants to be told that writing fiction is an endless round of revisions. Young bear, you'd better work just a bit harder at making writing interesting, or you're going to see more defections."

Baby Bear looked at his watch. "We actually only have about two minutes left before this workshop ends. And the next item on the schedule is the keynote address in the main auditorium. So your homework for tonight is to look back over your first five steps of the Snowflake and fix up anything that needs reworking. Finish your one-page synopsis, and then write up half a page to a full page on each of your characters. I want you to really get inside their skins. Explore their backstory. Figure out what makes them tick. Tomorrow, we'll—"

The bell rang.

Instantly, about half the students jumped up and grabbed their things and hurried for the door. The other half had been taking notes, and they took longer to leave.

Goldilocks felt horrible for Baby Bear. He must feel very discouraged to see so many of his students who didn't seem interested in what he was teaching. She followed him out of the classroom and down the hall.

He ducked inside the men's room.

Goldilocks didn't want to look like a stalker, so she kept walking toward the auditorium. But she wasn't much interested in hearing the keynote speaker.

She walked outside of the main building toward the coffee shop. She thought she heard voices from the back patio, so she peered around the shrubbery that blocked it off from sight.

The Big Bad Wolf was sitting at a table in the far corner drinking a large coffee.

Little Pig was pacing back and forth in front of him, arguing.

Goldilocks couldn't hear what he was saying, but Little Pig's face was very pink.

The Big Bad Wolf looked extremely angry.

Goldilocks didn't want to get involved, so she backed away and scurried to the parking lot and drove home, thinking about her story.

That evening, after the children were put to bed, she stayed up late going over everything she had done so far. She revised the one-paragraph summaries for each of the main characters. She finished her one-page synopsis. And she wrote up a full page on the backstory and motivations of each of her characters.

By the time she finished, it was very late. A little voice in her head told her that she shouldn't put so much work into these early parts. After all, she would only come back and revise them later.

But she had a hunch that the better job she did in the early steps, the less work she'd have in the later ones.

Tomorrow, she would talk to the Big Bad Wolf again and ask him just how interested he was in having her as a client. She thought he might be a very good agent to work with.

An agent with sharp teeth to show to the world, but a soft and kind heart inside.

Chapter Eleven

YOUR LONG SYNOPSIS

*G*oldilocks was the first person in the classroom the next morning. She hoped the Big Bad Wolf would arrive early, too, so she could talk to him about possibly being his client. Or Baby Bear, so she could show him her latest revisions.

But the second person to arrive was Little Pig. He walked straight toward the seat next to Goldilocks and sat down. "Did you get all your homework done last night?"

Goldilocks nodded and began to tell him of the surprises she'd found as she dug deep into each of her characters.

Little Pig nodded wisely as she talked. He seemed very interested in her story and asked several questions.

Before Goldilocks knew it, Baby Bear was rapping on the front table with his paws. "Good morning! I can see that there are fewer of you here today, but those who are here are the ones willing to put in the hard work. I'm proud of you all."

Goldilocks looked around to see who was there.

The room was only about two-thirds full.

The Big Bad Wolf walked in sipping a large coffee. He gave

Goldilocks a little wave, then scowled at Little Pig and found a seat near the back.

"Today, in the sixth step of the Snowflake," said Baby Bear, "we'll return to the plot of our stories. Remember that we alternate between characters and plot, characters and plot. That helps ensure that as we grow up our story, it's balanced."

"Dude, are we going to write a synopsis one of these days?" asked a young man in the second row. He was wearing an all-leather outfit, complete with a large bow and a quiver full of arrows. "Because I hear that's like the most important thing when you're trying to sell a book."

Baby Bear squinted at his name tag and then beamed at him. "Yes, Mr. Hood. Today, we'll take the one-page synopsis that you wrote yesterday and expand each paragraph out to about a full page. That should give you four or five pages, which I call the long synopsis."

"And we'll use this for what, exactly?" said Little Pig.

"Several things," said Baby Bear. "First, it helps you understand your story better. It makes you flesh out the details. You may find plot problems to be solved. You may find your theme emerging. You may see your characters getting deeper."

Goldilocks was taking notes on her laptop under the main heading PURPOSE OF LONG SYNOPSIS. She typed: *1) Flesh out story.*

"Second," said Baby Bear, "the long synopsis will help you when we get to step 8 of the Snowflake, in which you'll make a list of your scenes."

Goldilocks typed: *2) Prepare for scene list.*

Little Pig was drumming his hoof rapidly on the desktop. "Yes, but what about this business of selling the book?"

Baby Bear pointed to the back of the room. "Since we have a very prominent agent with us, I'll let the Big Bad Wolf talk about the importance of synopses."

The Big Bad Wolf stood up and took a long sip of his coffee. "Synopses are boring. Editors hate reading them. Agents hate reading them. What we like reading is your actual story—that's the fun part. But you *have* to write a synopsis or we won't even look at your story. Don't ask me why. It's a dumb tradition. So the first rule of writing a synopsis is this: shorter is better."

Goldilocks raised her hand. "If shorter is better, why do outliners write hundred-page synopses?"

"Because outliners *need* a ten-page or fifty-page or hundred-page synopsis just to write their first draft," said Baby Bear. "Writing the synopsis is part of their creative paradigm. They write the synopsis for their own benefit. But they don't send that huge synopsis to their agent and editor."

The Big Bad Wolf looked horrified. "If you send me an enormous synopsis, I'll burn it. I want to see at least two pages, no more than four. Period."

"So the third use of your long synopsis," Baby Bear said, "is to give you the raw material for the synopsis you'll send your agent."

Goldilocks typed: *3) Raw material for synopsis for agent.*

Little Pig cleared his throat. "So you're telling us to do all this work on a long synopsis just ... so we can do *more* work?" He sounded very irritated.

"I'm telling you that the long synopsis is a useful step on the way to understanding your story," said Baby Bear. "And a useful step on the way to writing a proposal for your agent."

"Time is money," said Little Pig. "This sort of busywork might be fine for the little people, but—"

"Tonight's homework," Baby Bear interrupted, "for those of you who don't consider the job *beneath* you, is to write a long synopsis for your novel. Just expand out the story in your short one-page synopsis, and you'll find that your long synopsis practically writes itself."

"Say, Goldilocks," said Little Pig. "I've been watching you, and you're quite a writer. Very gifted. How would you like to work with me on an amazing story, based on the life of an amazing pig?"

Goldilocks wasn't sure whether to laugh or to cry or to run screaming for the door.

"She's not interested," said the Big Bad Wolf.

Little Pig's head spun around. "Who asked you? I'm talking to Goldilocks. She's good at this sort of thing—"

"You're basically saying she's one of the little people who are good at busywork." The Big Bad Wolf glared at Little Pig. "Goldilocks is a talented writer, and she's got bigger fish to fry than to work on a stupid egomaniac's personal-experience story, thinly disguised as a novel."

Little Pig stood up. "You just see her as another cog in your empire. You want to take advantage of her and charge your outlandish agent fees while she does all the work. But what if her story never sells?"

"It'll sell," said the Big Bad Wolf. "Which is more than I can say for your stupid story. The best place for that is the *National Enquirer.*"

"The *National Enquirer?*" shrieked Little Pig. "Over my dead body!"

The Big Bad Wolf grinned maliciously. "That can be arranged, little piggie."

"Stop it, both of you!" Goldilocks shouted. She pointed a finger at the Big Bad Wolf. "You shouldn't say things like that. You need to apologize."

"Sorry." The Big Bad Wolf didn't look a bit sorry.

"And as for you ..." Goldilocks looked at Little Pig. "You have insulted me and demeaned me in every possible way. You are the last person I would ever coauthor a book with, and that's final!"

Little Pig's face ran through a rapid series of expressions. Shock. Rage. Humiliation. Cold fury. "Fine. You've had your chance. I'm out of here. If there are any other writers who want an excellent opportunity to work with a demanding yet good-hearted pig at a very reasonable level of pay, I'll be in the coffee shop for the next hour."

He stomped out of the classroom, leaving little black hoof marks on the tile floor.

The room sat in uneasy silence for a few seconds.

"Well," said Baby Bear. "It takes all kinds. Little Pig is one of those that it takes all kinds of. Now, is your homework assignment clear?"

All the students nodded.

Baby Bear looked straight at the Big Bad Wolf. "You were a bit harsh on him, you know. You really ought to … let things go."

The Big Bad Wolf scowled. "He lied about me on the witness stand about some threats I supposedly made against his brothers. That took six years out of my life. Be my guest, Baby Bear. You go do time in the Big House for a crime you didn't commit, and then you can come and talk to me about letting things go. Until then, forget it."

Goldilocks was trying to make sense of all this. The Big Bad Wolf had been convicted … on Little Pig's testimony? Was it Little Pig's brothers he'd been accused of murdering?

"In any event," said Baby Bear, "we've discussed the long synopsis, and now I want to cover character bibles. That will be step 7 of the Snowflake. After that, we still have three steps in the Snowflake Method, and we need to get through those because we'll be wrapping up the conference tomorrow afternoon."

"Dude, don't we get, like, a break or something?" said the young man in the second row.

Baby Bear checked his watch. "I *suppose*, but we really need to keep moving. You can all take a five-minute break, but please don't loiter. We still have a lot of ground to cover."

Goldilocks had been planning to talk to the Big Bad Wolf

during the break. But she felt so shocked by his bad-tempered outburst over Little Pig that she was having second thoughts. She didn't want an agent who would be hard to work with, and the Big Bad Wolf clearly had a dark side.

Chapter Twelve

YOUR CHARACTER BIBLE

*D*uring the break, Goldilocks hurried down the hall to the snack table and got a banana and a cup of tea. She smiled at the young man with the bow and arrows. "What sort of novel are you writing?"

He gave her a confident grin. "It's a collection of tales about a band of merry outlaws living in the forest, shooting wild deer and drinking ale and kissing wenches and evading the local sheriff."

"Well, good luck on that ..." Goldilocks peered at his name tag. "... um, Robin. Your story sounds awesome."

He shrugged modestly. "Your story is pretty epic, too. I hope Baby Bear puts you on the hot seat again. I learn, like, loads about writing every time he gets you up there." His eyes flicked down to her chest for a moment, and a sloppy smile played across his face. "And you look like a wench who likes to have fun. If you ever want to hang out in the forest—"

"Oh, my!" Goldilocks pointed to her watch. "Look at the time. We'd better get back to our workshop."

When they reached the classroom, the Big Bad Wolf was curled up on the floor in the back corner of the classroom, snoring gently.

Precisely on time, Baby Bear rapped on the front table. "Step 7 in the Snowflake Method is to write up a character bible for each of your characters. You can do this however it works best for you. Some authors like to start by finding pictures on the Internet that resemble their characters. If that helps you visualize your character, then do it. But let's remember the most important thing. You want to know enough about your characters so that you can get inside their skins."

Baby Bear passed out sheets of paper with a large number of questions.

Robin looked at his and started snickering. "Why do I need to know what color my hero's eyes are?"

Goldilocks couldn't believe he could be so ignorant. "That's important! You can tell a lot about a character from the color of his eyes."

Robin laughed out loud. "What can you tell about me?"

She studied him. "Your eyes are all red and bloodshot. I bet you drink loads of ale and stay out too late at night chasing loose women."

"Wenches," he said. "Not loose women. Wenches."

Goldilocks sniffed. "Same difference."

Baby Bear cleared his throat. "You're both missing an important point here. All too many books show the heroine with blue eyes on page 1 and green eyes on page 99. One purpose of your character bible is to give you a place to save all the little details about each character—so you don't make mistakes like that."

"Who would be so stupid?" asked Goldilocks.

"It happens all the time," said Baby Bear.

"Why can't you just remember that sort of thing?"

"When it's 3:00 a.m. on the day your book is due to your editor, and you're reading the proofs one last time to be sure it's perfect, you'll be very glad you have one central place where you can look up what year the village postmistress was born."

Goldilocks frowned. "Has that ever happened to you?"

"Every book," Baby Bear said. "It's nice to be able to find it in one minute, not ten."

"There's nothing in your list of questions about what kind of nail polish my heroine wears," said Goldilocks.

"Heavens!" said Mrs. Hubbard. "Who can afford nail polish?"

Robin snickered. "More important, who would wear it? That is, like, the most shallow question I can imagine."

"Nail polish is important!" Goldilocks said. "It says a lot about your character."

Robin scoffed. "Tell me what brand of ale a man drinks, and I'll tell you whether he's a good man or a lackey of the Sheriff of Nottingham. That's the important thing."

"Speaking of *shallow*," Goldilocks said.

Baby Bear held up his paws. "Peace, people! If you look at the questions on this list, you'll see some that seem useful to you and some that don't. If a question simply doesn't apply to your character, then ignore it. If there are other questions not on the list that would help you understand your characters better, then add them."

"It seems like loads of work," said Robin.

"It is a *lot* of work," said Baby Bear. "I often take a full working day for each of my main characters. But it's time well spent. I suggest we put Goldilocks on the hot seat and quiz her a bit about some of her characters."

The room began buzzing with excitement.

Goldilocks went up to the front and sat on the hot seat. She knew that this wasn't going to be easy, but she also knew it would be valuable.

Baby Bear studied Goldilocks for a moment. "Part of your novel takes place in Elise's home. Describe it."

She stared at him. "But … aren't all houses pretty much alike?"

"Suppose you tell me what your house is like," said Baby Bear.

Goldilocks frowned. "I'm sure it's just like anyone else's. It's a nice three-bedroom house on a sixth-of-an-acre lot. The exterior is stucco and the roof is tile, and there's an attached two-car garage. The windows are triple-paned—"

"That's not a house, that's a prison," said Robin. "Goldilocks, you have, like, totally subjugated yourself to the Man."

"Robin, tell us about your house," Baby Bear said.

He shrugged. "It's a cave out in Sherwood Forest. I live there with my band of merry men. There's no windows to keep in the smoke when we roast the wild deer we poached from the sheriff's lands. Nothing artificial. We are, like, the original Thoreau. It's awesome!"

"Is the cupboard bare?" asked Mrs. Hubbard. "That's what my house is like, and I think it's just fascinating."

Robin Hood shook his head. "We don't have cupboards, but our cook fires are never bare. If you want a little excitement, you can come check us out. And bring some of your wench friends."

Mrs. Hubbard's cheeks turned pink, and she giggled. "I might just do that, young man. I'll bring my granddaughter, Marian. I think she's exactly your type." She looked at Baby Bear. "What is your house like, young bear?"

Baby Bear didn't say anything.

"I'll bet it's a rustic little thatched cottage far out in the woods," said Goldilocks. "With a wooden table and three wooden bowls for porridge. And three wooden chairs. And upstairs, three beds— one too hard, one too soft, and one just right."

Baby Bear gave her a curious look. "How would you know all that?"

Goldilocks felt her cheeks turning hot. "Oh! Was I right? I was, you know, just guessing."

"You have … quite an imagination." Baby Bear looked like he wanted to say something else, but then he shook his head. "So I want you to apply that imagination to your character, Elise. What is her house like?"

Goldilocks was glad to get back to Elise. "Well, of course it has three bedrooms and two bathrooms. There's a nice quiet study upstairs for Elise to write her novels. And there's a kitchen on the first floor with a lovely marble countertop and a huge cooking island right in the center."

Mrs. Hubbard began laughing. "Dearie, what planet are you living on? Nobody had a house like that in the 1940s."

"They … didn't?" Goldilocks said. "Well, I suppose Elise's house would be smaller. Two bedrooms and one bath, then."

Mrs. Hubbard just shook her head. "Honey, you need to do a little research. Your character lives in a little village in France in 1944. Are you sure they even *have* a bathroom in the house? And whatever happened to the parlor?"

"Parlor?" Goldilocks said. "Why would they have a parlor and not a bathroom?"

"Oh, mercy, you have some homework to do," said the old woman. "You need to look at pictures of actual houses from that time and place. See what we had to work with back when I was just a lass."

The door opened and a photographer came in. He was young and geeky and dressed all in black, with a silver ring in his nose. He was carrying a huge, expensive camera, which he aimed at Baby Bear. "The conference director wants some shots of you and your class. Stand next to your student there and act like you're teaching her or something."

Baby Bear came and stood awkwardly beside Goldilocks. Even though she was sitting down, he was still shorter than her.

"Cheese," said Goldilocks.

"Porridge," said Baby Bear.

The photographer took several shots in quick succession. Then he circled around the two of them, taking pictures from all possible angles.

After he left, Baby Bear scratched his head. "Where were we? Ah, yes. You have some research to do on the layout of villagers' homes in 1944 France."

"But … why?" Goldilocks said. "I can just make things up, can't I? It's fiction."

"Don't forget the jet car in the garage," said Robin.

Goldilocks glared at him. "What kind of idiot would put a jet car in a garage? Nobody has jet cars! They aren't invented yet."

"Exactly," said Mrs. Hubbard.

Baby Bear stepped in. "You're quite right, Robin and Mrs. Hubbard. Houses were very different in 1944, and Goldilocks can't just make things up. She needs to do some research. This is important, because there'll be a lot of action in Elise's house, and the layout of the building will determine what kind of action is possible."

Goldilocks was beginning to see it. "Oh, because if I have a fight scene in the kitchen and there's no island in the center, then I can't have them bashing each other against it or dodging around it."

"Exactly."

"Oh, my! This is a *lot* of work!" said Goldilocks.

"We've hardly begun," said Baby Bear. "But perhaps we should ask the Big Bad Wolf to come up and help us brainstorm about your …"

Baby Bear stopped. He was scanning all around the room with a strange expression on his face.

Goldilocks stood up and looked to the far back corner where she had seen the Big Bad Wolf sleeping earlier.

The Big Bad Wolf was gone.

The room was silent for a long moment.

From far away, a shrill note began rising and falling, rising and falling, louder and louder.

Goldilocks's heart began slamming against her chest.

The sound was the distant wail of an ambulance.

Chapter Thirteen

YOUR THIRD DISASTER

"*E*verybody stay in your seats," Baby Bear said. "I need to check on something." He hurried to the door and flung it open.

The wail of the ambulance poured into the room.

Baby Bear sprinted out into the hallway, slamming the door shut behind him.

The class began buzzing.

Goldilocks felt like her head was filled with sand.

Somebody tapped her on the shoulder. It was Mrs. Hubbard. "Dearie, would you put in a word for me with that lovely fellow, the Big Bad Wolf? I was hoping to ask him to look at my manuscript."

Goldilocks didn't know what to say. "Did anyone see the Big Bad Wolf go out?"

"We were all watching you," said Robin. "Goldilocks, you are, like, one amazing wench."

A police siren sounded, far away, hurtling toward them.

Goldilocks felt like she was going to lose her breakfast.

The door flew open and Baby Bear staggered in. "I have some

very bad news. There's been a … murder over at the coffee shop. Little Pig is dead. Papa Bear has made a citizen's arrest."

"Who was it, dude?" asked Robin. "I bet it was the Big Bad Wolf, am I right?"

Tears stood out in Baby Bear's eyes. "I just … can't believe it. I was so sure he'd reformed."

Goldilocks gasped. "Oh, my!" She felt numb all over. This couldn't be true. She knew the Big Bad Wolf. He was a very nice wolf. She felt certain he had been joking when he made those threatening comments.

Mrs. Hubbard began sobbing softly. "That Little Pig was such a nice young pig."

Then suddenly, the whole class was on their feet and surging toward the door.

Goldilocks joined in the rush to get out.

"Wait, everybody!" shouted Baby Bear. "The police will need you to make statements."

But nobody was listening.

Somebody jostled Goldilocks from behind.

She tripped and fell.

Strong paws gripped Goldilocks and pulled her to one side, out of the rush of trampling feet.

In a moment, the room was empty except for Goldilocks and Baby Bear.

"Thank you for rescuing me," Goldilocks said.

The door flew open and Mama Bear staggered in. "Oh, this is perfectly dreadful! I can't believe what's happened. I knew you should never have brought that terrible wolf to help out in your classes, Baby Bear. You know what sort of family he comes from, not to mention his record. And now this!" She wrung her paws dramatically and began sobbing.

Baby Bear shook his head, a perplexed look on his face. "I don't see how this could have happened. The Big Bad Wolf was napping in the corner. He must have slipped out while I was working with Goldilocks."

"Oh, it's just horrible, horrible!" Mama Bear sniffled loudly and wiped her nose with the back of her paw. "The police are questioning the Big Bad Wolf right now. We'll be ruined when word gets out that it was you who invited him to the conference."

Goldilocks began trembling. "Do you think it's ... quite certain he killed Little Pig?"

Baby Bear put his laptop into his backpack. "Papa Bear doesn't make mistakes. If he arrested the Big Bad Wolf, then ... he's absolutely certain he's guilty."

"But what do *you* think?" Goldilocks said. "Could he have done it?"

"I just ... don't know," said Baby Bear. "He's a well-mannered wolf, but he *is* a wolf. He was convicted of murdering Little Pig's two brothers years ago. And Papa Bear says he caught him practically red-handed. So the evidence is very strong."

"Evidence, shmevidence," said Mama Bear. "What do you *feel*? Do you *feel* in your heart that he's a killer?"

Baby Bear's face sagged. "Maybe," he said in a very small voice. "I hate to say it, but yes, I think he did it. Again."

Goldilocks fanned her face. If even Baby Bear thought the Big Bad Wolf had done it, then ... she had to face the facts. The Big Bad Wolf was guilty.

The conference director came in. She was a short, stout woman with gray hair and a severe face. "You all are needed for questioning. The police want to know what you saw and when you saw it."

The bears and Goldilocks went out and walked down the long tiled hallway to the doors. Outside, several police cars had pulled up on the sidewalk near the coffee shop and sat parked at odd angles with their blue-and-red lights flashing. There was yellow crime scene tape across the front door of the coffee shop and all around the patio in back.

Goldilocks moved closer to see what had happened.

There was a large crowd gathered there, gawking and murmuring.

Papa Bear was surrounded by policemen. His voice boomed out. "I've told you this six times. I went in to buy coffee, and then walked out through the side door onto the back patio. I saw Little Pig lying on the concrete, stabbed to death. There was blood everywhere, and wolf tracks in the mud by the body. I went running back to the conference center building and found the Big Bad Wolf in the men's room washing his paws."

Two burly policemen came out of the coffee shop, leading the Big Bad Wolf. He was handcuffed, and two more policemen were walking behind him, guns drawn.

The Big Bad Wolf's eyes were red and swollen, and his face looked paralyzed with fear.

Goldilocks thought he might have been crying.

"Move along, people, nothing to see here," said one of the cops. He led the way to a police car and opened the back door.

The Big Bad Wolf staggered along in a daze.

A policeman put his hand on top of the Big Bad Wolf's head and pushed him down into the car. Two cops got in the backseat on either side of him. The other two got in the front.

The siren started, and the car pushed forward through the crowd.

"He … I don't think he did it!" Goldilocks said. "Did you see his face?"

"I saw it," Papa Bear growled. "If ever I've seen a guilty look on a wolf's face, it was right there."

Mama Bear joined them, and her whole body shook with sobs. "This is just horrible, horrible! And to think that our son knows him! We'll be ruined."

Baby Bear frowned at them. "*We'll* be ruined? Nonsense. It's the Big Bad Wolf who'll be ruined. He's been working so hard to build his client list. And now he's going back to prison. He'll never get out after a second murder rap."

"But … how do we know for sure he did it?" Goldilocks said.

The three bears stared at her.

Goldilocks felt very foolish, but she had to stand up for what she thought. "What if he's innocent?" she said.

Papa Bear shook his head. "Miss Goldilocks, you're obviously very young and inexperienced. If anything is certain, it's that the Big Bad Wolf killed Little Pig."

"Oh, if only you had never invited this horrible wolf to the conference!" Mama Bear shook her paw at Baby Bear.

"Well, I couldn't have known he was going to kill Little Pig," Baby Bear said angrily. "I thought he was reformed."

"He's a wolf, son," said Papa Bear. "Wolves don't change. If you're wicked, then you're wicked right through, and nothing is going to change who you are."

He was looking right at Goldilocks when he said this.

Goldilocks felt so guilty she thought she was going to explode.

"You look familiar," said Mama Bear. "Haven't I seen you before?"

Goldilocks felt her whole body turn hot. "I … I was in your workshop the other day—the one on organic writing."

"Ah." Mama Bear fixed a skeptical eye on her. "I could swear I've seen you somewhere else, a long time ago."

Goldilocks wanted to run and hide. But she'd been running and hiding all her life, and she was tired of it. "I … I have a confession to make. Years ago, I … went out for a long walk in the woods. I came to a small cottage and went inside. I was horribly hungry and I ate some food. Then I broke one of the chairs and fell asleep in one of the beds."

"You!" shouted Papa Bear. "You're the criminal!"

"I … I want to make it right," Goldilocks said. "I want to pay for the damage I did."

"I'll have you arrested." Papa Bear spun around and waved toward the police officers still on the scene.

None of them seemed to notice him.

Goldilocks felt like she had drunk a pitcher of ice water.

"Now, Papa." Mama Bear moved forward and wrapped up Goldilocks in a huge, furry hug. "She was just a young girl. And she's lived with the guilt all these years. Surely, if she pays for the damage, that will be all anyone could ask."

"Perhaps she had a horrible childhood," Baby Bear said. "Perhaps she was lost. Or hungry. Or frightened of bears. There could be … all sorts of reasons she did what she did."

"Harrumph! She should have gone to jail." Papa Bear scowled at Goldilocks.

"I'm very sorry for what I did," Goldilocks said. "I'll pay for the damage."

"Well … of course, I kept the receipts for repairs," Papa Bear said. "In a file in my office. A tax deduction, you know. There's a line item for losses due to crime."

"I … feel so awful about it," Goldilocks said.

"It's quite all right, dear." Mama Bear patted her heavily on the back. "If you knew some of the shenanigans Baby Bear got into as a young bear—"

Baby Bear cleared his throat. "Goldilocks, if you really don't think the Big Bad Wolf is guilty, then I suggest you go visit him and get his side of the story. Because as of right now, you're the only person who thinks he's innocent."

She nodded. "Of course. I'm sorry I'll miss your class after lunch."

"There won't be any classes this afternoon," Mama Bear said. "I've already spoken with the conference director, and they're canceling all workshops for the afternoon. The police will need to talk to everybody, especially you, Baby Bear."

Papa Bear was still frowning. "You ought to have known what

sort of family he came from, son. Murder is in his genes, in his blood. You can't change what you are."

Goldilocks didn't believe him. She knew people could change. Wolves could change too.

She had to visit the Big Bad Wolf and get his side of the story.

*T*hat afternoon, Goldilocks went to visit the Big Bad Wolf. She had to wait a long time at the local jail.

An unpleasant female cop searched her roughly for weapons before allowing her into the visitation room.

Goldilocks sat down in a painful plastic chair at a long, cheap Formica-topped table that split the room in half from one wall to the other. A ceiling-high glass partition ran down the middle of the table. The room was empty and smelled like dirty gym socks and mildew. Goldilocks waited for a quarter of an hour before the door opened.

The Big Bad Wolf shuffled in, staring at the floor, handcuffed and shackled, wearing an orange jumpsuit. His face looked haggard. He slumped into his seat and only then looked at his visitor. "Oh, it's you!" He hung his head. "I'm sorry. I suppose you think I'm a horrible person."

Goldilocks wanted to hug him. "I think you're a good and kind wolf. I think there's been a terrible mistake. I don't believe you killed Little Pig."

The Big Bad Wolf's eyebrows shot up for just an instant. "You don't?"

"Absolutely not. You couldn't have. You aren't that kind of wolf."

"I don't have any alibi to prove I didn't. What makes you think I'm innocent?"

"Because you're kind," said Goldilocks. "You care about people. You help people with their writing. I know you make jokes about eating little pigs, but they're only jokes. So tell me what really happened."

"I was sleeping and having a terrible dream," said the Big Bad Wolf. "There was a little pig making rude comments about me. Old Mother Hubbard was complaining about her bare cupboard. Some idiot in a Robin Hood suit was making crude remarks to young wenches. And then I woke up and needed to use the men's room. I had a big latte this morning, and ... um ..."

"I get it, I get it." Goldilocks blushed.

"Baby Bear had you up front on the hot seat talking about something or other, and I just slipped out through the back door and went to the men's room. Then I was washing my paws when Papa Bear burst in, saw me, started shouting horrible things, and threw me on the floor. He sat on top of me and called 911. The next thing I knew, the police were there. They took me over to the coffee shop, way around to the back patio. They made me look at that poor Little Pig, stabbed to death in the back corner, lying in a pool of blood. Then they started shouting at me."

Tears began streaming down the Big Bad Wolf's face. "They asked if I had any idea what might have happened to him. Asked if I had any thoughts on who the killer might be. I think they were trying to make me confess before they formally arrested me and read me my rights. But I had nothing to confess. So they brought me here and spent two hours interrogating me."

"That's horrible," Goldilocks said.

"Did anybody in the class see me when I left the room?" asked the Big Bad Wolf. "Because Papa Bear arrested me only a minute or two after that."

Goldilocks shook her head. "I didn't. Baby Bear didn't. I think everybody was watching him and me up front, but I'll ask around and see if anyone saw you leave."

"All the evidence is against me. It's circumstantial evidence, but I don't have an alibi and I do have a record. I don't stand a chance. Nobody believes me. Even my lawyer doesn't believe me."

"I believe you." Goldilocks stood up and leaned forward as close to the glass partition as she could. "There's got to be a way to prove you're innocent, and I'm going to find it."

"Are you sure you want to do that?" the Big Bad Wolf said. "It's going to ruin your reputation. People are going to wonder why you're standing up for me. People are going to talk about you. They might even start looking into your past, and—"

"I don't care what people think!" Goldilocks said. "I'm going to do what I think is right, and if people think ill of me, that's their problem."

The Big Bad Wolf simply stared at her. A look of awe shone in his gleaming eyes. "You've ... changed, Goldilocks. Just a few days ago, you were letting other people's opinions dictate your life."

"You better believe I've changed, and you helped me do it. When you shot Baby Bear, I decided that nothing was going to stop me from being a writer. And then when Little Pig told me you were going to reject me, I realized that I had to stand up for my story, even if it cost me my chance to land a famous agent."

The Big Bad Wolf was counting on his fingers. "Those are two disasters. Now here's a third disaster—I'm accused of murder—and you're committing to defend me at any cost. How do you feel right now?"

"Terrified," said Goldilocks. "Excited. Foolish. Ready to throw myself wholeheartedly into the battle and win."

"Remember that feeling," said the Big Bad Wolf. "Lock it away in your heart. That is exactly the way Elise is going to feel at her third disaster, when she rescues Monique and Dirk gets badly wounded. She could run away, but she resolves to help blow up the ammo dump and help win the war. She's committing to an ending, happy, sad, or bittersweet."

Goldilocks was trembling. "Elise's story is just like my story, isn't it?"

"That's what story is for," said the Big Bad Wolf. "Story teaches you how to do the right thing. By living inside the skins of characters who do the right thing, you develop the emotional muscle memory to do the right thing yourself."

A guard appeared at the door and stabbed a finger at Goldilocks. "Time!"

She stood up and headed toward the door, then turned and blew the Big Bad Wolf a kiss. "I won't let you down."

He managed a weak grin. "Succeed or fail, you've already won."

The guard hauled Goldilocks out, and the heavy metal door slammed shut.

Goldilocks hadn't missed the look of anguish on the wolf's face. He was proud of her for wanting to help. But it was obvious that he thought she was going to fail.

The Big Bad Wolf had given up hope.

Chapter Fourteen

YOUR LIST OF SCENES

That evening, after the children went to bed, Goldilocks sat up late thinking. Was there some way to prove that the Big Bad Wolf could not have killed Little Pig?

She opened a document and began typing.

First, she wrote up a character sheet on the Big Bad Wolf. His Goal, she already knew, was to become the world's greatest literary agent. From that, she could guess his Ambition. He wanted to be an important person in the literary world. She wasn't sure of his Values, but she made some guesses.

Nothing is more important than survival.
Nothing is more important than honor.
Nothing is more important than helping others.

She couldn't see how killing Little Pig would be in line with any of those Values.

But that wasn't proof. That was simply her fuzzy-minded novelist's brain making an emotional judgment. She was behaving like Mama Bear.

Papa Bear would look at things more rationally. He'd make an outline of the Big Bad Wolf's life story.

Goldilocks began typing up a rough synopsis of the events in the Big Bad Wolf's life.

Growing up knowing that his uncle had eaten Little Red's grandmother. Getting framed for murder. Going to jail because of the lying testimony of Little Pig. Living in fear of the thugs in prison. Learning to be tough to survive. Finally getting paroled. Going out on the streets. Making the decision to become an agent. Attending writer's conferences. Helping Baby Bear teach his class. Getting into an argument with Little Pig in the coffee shop.

Goldilocks shook her head. Her synopsis was all about actions. It didn't get inside the skin of the Big Bad Wolf. And it made great leaps from one event to another, without showing the connections.

She was getting a headache and it was very late, and she suddenly realized that she hadn't yet done her homework. She wanted so very badly to go to bed and sleep and forget everything. But she also wanted very badly to be a novelist. She wanted to complete her novel. She wanted the Big Bad Wolf to be her agent.

She knew that sounded foolish, because everybody said he was a murderer. But she couldn't shake her belief that deep inside, he had a good, kind heart. Today, he'd been more concerned about her reputation than his.

Goldilocks felt very tired, but she opened her Snowflake document and expanded her one-page synopsis to four pages. Then she rapidly typed out character bibles for her main characters.

By the time she finished, it was after 3:00 a.m., and her head felt muzzy. She staggered into bed and slept like the dead.

*M*orning came far too soon. Goldilocks grabbed a hasty breakfast, took her children to school, and raced over to the conference center. She dashed into the classroom five minutes late.

Baby Bear scowled at her. "Well, it seems that everyone is *finally* here. Let's begin. But first, a word about what happened yesterday. It looks like I made a terrible error in judgment in inviting the Big Bad Wolf to come help me at this conference. I thought he had reformed, but I was horribly, tragically wrong. I don't know how I'm going to live with myself, knowing that I'm responsible for the murder of Little Pig."

"You don't know that!" Goldilocks said. "The Big Bad Wolf says he didn't do it."

"Well, dude, it's not like he's going to admit anything," said Robin Hood. "Of course he claims he didn't do it. But we know for sure he's murdered pigs before."

"He was framed before, and now he's being framed again," Goldilocks said stubbornly.

"Oh, like that is totally logical," Robin Hood sneered.

"I'd think you of all people ought to understand," Goldilocks said. "Didn't the Sheriff of Nottingham ever accuse you of something you didn't do?"

Robin Hood's mouth fell open. "All the time. He's, like, the Man, the oppressor of the people."

"Well, what if the Man is oppressing the Big Bad Wolf? Isn't that possible?"

Robin Hood just looked at her. "I ... suppose it is. That's what the Man does—oppresses people. And Little Pig, if you ask me, was in the back pocket of the Man. What do we know about him?"

Baby Bear began pacing. "Little Pig was a very wealthy businessman. He started the business years ago with his two brothers, and took over full control after they were tragically murdered. He has no children, but there is a nephew, a young fellow from New

York, who has arrived in town and is demanding the death penalty for the Big Bad Wolf."

"Aren't there any witnesses?" Goldilocks said. "Maybe a security camera in the coffee shop?"

Baby Bear shook his head. "There's a security camera trained on the coffee shop back patio, but it's broken. The conference center isn't wired, and there weren't any witnesses."

"The Big Bad Wolf said he left here only a minute or two before Papa Bear found him in the men's room," Goldilocks said. "That's not enough time to kill Little Pig. Papa Bear was there at the coffee shop. He'd have seen him."

Robin Hood took an arrow out of his quiver and began tapping the point with his fingers. "We've got no proof of when the Big Bad Wolf left. Didn't anybody see him go out?"

Heads shook all around the room.

"Well, I'm afraid his record is against him," Mrs. Hubbard said. "If you ask me, a bent tree never grows straight."

Baby Bear studied Goldilocks for a long moment. "I ... suppose not everyone would agree with that. But the fact is that even without hard evidence, any jury is going to convict the Big Bad Wolf just because of who he is. Now, I know this is difficult, but let's shift gears to talk about writing. Did any of you complete the homework?"

Mrs. Hubbard raised her hand. "I wrote a long character bible on my main character, who is a poor but honest widow. I have an excellent description of her cupboard."

"Let me guess," said Robin Hood. "It's ... bare?"

"You're so smart!" Mrs. Hubbard said admiringly.

"It's a nice start," Baby Bear said. "Did you do your other characters?"

"What other characters?" Mrs. Hubbard asked. "I only have the one. The whole story is about her bare cupboard."

"And did you write a four-page synopsis?" Baby Bear asked.

Mrs. Hubbard sighed deeply. "Young bear, you really are

asking a lot. I got my synopsis up to a page and a quarter. There's only so much you can say about a cupboard."

"Perhaps what you've got there is a short story, rather than a full-length novel," Baby Bear said. "Who wrote all their character bibles *and* their four-page synopsis?"

Goldilocks raised her hand, and then looked to see who else had done it.

Not a single other hand was raised.

Mrs. Hubbard was staring at Goldilocks with a look of astonishment.

Robin Hood was studying her appreciatively, his eyes running from her face all the way down her body to her long, slim legs, and then back up again. He winked at her and smiled.

Baby Bear frowned. "There's a reason only a few writers get their novels published. You need to discipline yourselves to do the work. It's hard work, but if you don't do it, you aren't behaving professionally. Apparently, only one of you has done what's necessary, and she looks a little ragged today. I was planning to give her a break, but it looks like I don't have much choice. Goldilocks, please come up to the hot seat."

Goldilocks staggered a little on the way forward. She hadn't done much with her hair this morning, and she'd probably done a horrible job on her makeup. Baby Bear must think she was very unprofessional.

"Let me just look at your homework." Baby Bear pointed to her laptop.

Goldilocks set it on the table. "My documents are both already open."

Baby Bear skimmed rapidly through her character bible and long synopsis. "Hmmm, this is quite good. Your synopsis is a little thin on the third page. I think you'll need to beef up the second half of your second act. And your ending feels very rushed."

"I'm sorry," Goldilocks said in a quiet voice. "I was trying so hard to think how to help the Big Bad Wolf that I didn't get started on my homework until after midnight. I was up till 3:00 a.m., and I know everything I wrote must be awful, but—"

"You wrote all this *after* midnight?" Baby Bear said. "That's ..."

A hiss of astonishment went around the room.

"Amazing," said a girl in the back row with a pierced eyebrow. "Goldilocks, you're like a rock star at this writing thing."

"Goldilocks has a terrific work ethic," Baby Bear said. "Which is why I think she has a good chance to succeed. This is excellent work, considering that she did it all so late last night. There are some things to improve, but this is the last day of the conference, and we really need to press on. So let's go to step 8 in the Snowflake Method. We need a list of scenes for her novel."

Goldilocks felt her head beginning to ache again. More work? Seriously? She massaged the back of her neck and hunched her shoulders. They felt stiff and sore.

"Are you all right, Goldilocks?" Baby Bear asked.

"I ... just feel terrible about the Big Bad Wolf," Goldilocks said. "And my head hurts and my shoulders are sore, and I'm wondering how much more work we have to do before I can start writing my novel."

Baby Bear gave her a sympathetic look. "I understand. You're tired, and you want to start writing. But is that realistic? If you started writing your novel today, would you know what to put in the very first scene?"

"No," Goldilocks said in a dejected voice. "That's always been my problem. I don't know how to get beyond the first word in my novel. I suppose I'm just a terrible writer." She felt so desperately discouraged that she wanted to give up and go home.

"You're a very good writer," said Baby Bear. "All you need is a bit more coaching, and things should become clear. Let's talk about how you're going to start your story. Your hero, Dirk, is going to break his leg parachuting into Elise's garden, right?"

"But don't I need to show all of Dirk's training as a commando?" Goldilocks said. "And about how Elise became a widow? And about Henri growing up and wanting to be respected by other people?"

"All of that is what we call 'backstory,'" Baby Bear said. "That's important information that *you* need to know so you understand your characters. But it's not necessary for your *reader* to know it just yet. You first have to get your target reader to care about your main story. Then she'll be dying to know your backstory. Your main story begins when Dirk meets Elise."

"Well, then, since Elise is my main character, shouldn't I start the first scene with her?"

"You could," Baby Bear said. "How would that scene look?"

"She'd, um, put her daughter Monique to bed, and then she'd sit quietly knitting by the lamp, and then she'd go to bed, and then around 3:00 a.m. she'd wake up because she heard a noise outside, and she'd go out to look, and there would be Dirk."

Baby Bear looked around the room. "Sounds pretty exciting, doesn't it? A quiet evening like every other quiet evening in the life of a lonely young widow. How many of you would find that fun to read?"

The other writers all sat studying their hands. Nobody said anything.

Baby Bear turned to Goldilocks. "Maybe you could start the story with a scene about Monique. Would that work?"

Goldilocks giggled. "But ... Monique just plays with her dolls until bedtime and then goes to bed and sleeps all night, and in the morning, she wakes up and Dirk is in the house. That's not interesting at all."

"Then we can't start with her, can we?" said Baby Bear. "Maybe Henri? What was he doing on the night Dirk arrived?"

Goldilocks realized she hadn't even thought about Henri. But she knew she must. He was an important character. "He went over to court Elise. Monique made him play dolls with her until her bedtime. After that, Henri sat on the love seat and talked about the war while Elise sat in the rocking chair by the kerosene lamp knitting. He wanted her to sit beside him, but she said she needed the light to see. Around midnight, he went home feeling very frustrated, wondering whether Elise really liked him."

Baby Bear shrugged his furry little shoulders. "Not terribly exciting, is it?"

Goldilocks felt a cold, hard knot forming in her belly. Her novel had seemed so wonderful until she actually tried to plan the first scene. Now it seemed boring.

"Tell me about how Dirk spent the evening," Baby Bear said.

Goldilocks thought for a few seconds. "It was a cold, rainy night. He and the other commandos dressed up all in black and packed their kits and loaded up into the plane. They were flying very high and very fast, hoping to avoid anti-aircraft fire. They were almost to their jump zone when a German fighter plane started chasing them. The American pilot swooped and dove and tried hard to evade, but the German shot up their wing and the engine caught fire. The commandos all ran to the door to get out. The jumpmaster pushed Dirk out first. Half a second later, the plane exploded above him. He saw plane parts and bodies falling in the light of the moon. Then he dropped into dense clouds. He waited as long as possible before opening his parachute, to avoid being strafed by ground fire. When he came out of the clouds, he was only a thousand feet above the ground. He yanked the ripcord and the chute jerked him upward. He saw that he was drifting toward a fence, and he barely managed to guide his chute into an open garden. The light was bad, and he misjudged the landing and hit hard on his right leg. It buckled, and he collapsed on the ground and lost consciousness."

The room had gone absolutely silent.

Goldilocks had been staring at her gold-flecked nails while she talked. She looked at Baby Bear.

He was smiling.

She looked at the class.

They were staring at her.

"That's terrific," said Baby Bear. "I think you've got a killer opening scene. It starts with a clear goal. There's plenty of conflict all the way through. And it ends with a setback."

"What do I need to do?" Goldilocks said.

"Open up a spreadsheet on your laptop and make a very wide first column and then type in what happens in the scene," said Baby Bear.

Goldilocks opened a spreadsheet and started typing. "There's not enough room here. I can't put in all those details."

"Can you summarize the scene in one sentence?" Baby Bear said.

"Yes, of course. Dirk and his fellow commandos are shot up as they near their drop zone, and Dirk breaks his leg when he lands badly in Elise's garden."

"Is that enough to remember everything else you said?"

"I'm sure it'll jog my memory," said Goldilocks. "That scene would be very hard to forget."

"Then you don't need any more than that," said Baby Bear. "Now your homework is to write one line in the spreadsheet for every scene in your novel. You can work from your long synopsis that you created in step 6 of the Snowflake. Focus on events that happen over a short period of time—minutes or a few hours. Just tell the main thing that happens in each scene."

"That's going to be a huge amount of work," said Mrs. Hubbard. "Why not just start writing?"

"You *can* just start writing if you want," said Baby Bear. "But if you don't know *what* to start writing yet, creating a scene list will help you figure that out."

Goldilocks was staring unhappily at her laptop.

"Is something wrong?" Baby Bear asked.

"It's just … I really hate spreadsheets," Goldilocks said. "They remind me of that horrible job I used to have. Why not just write all this in a Word document or a text file?"

"That's a very good question," said Baby Bear. "The reason is because you're going to be using more columns in the spread-sheet. Each scene has a point-of-view character. That's the char-acter whose head you're going to get inside for that scene. So you need a column in your spreadsheet to tell who the POV character is."

Goldilocks made a new column in her spreadsheet and typed in "Dirk" in the first row of the column. "Are there going to be any other columns?"

"That's up to you," said Baby Bear. "You might want a column that tells you how many words you expect for the scene. A short scene might be only five hundred words. A medium scene might be a thousand. A long scene might be two or even three thousand words."

"Why would I care about that?" asked Goldilocks.

"Because then you can add up all the numbers and estimate how long your book is going to be."

Goldilocks stared at him in disbelief. "That's crazy! I hate adding up numbers. And what if I change one of the numbers? Then I'd have to add them all up again."

Baby Bear sighed. "One of the things a spreadsheet can do very easily is to add up numbers. You just tell it to do that, and then if you ever change one of the numbers, the spreadsheet will auto-matically recalculate the total. So you'll always know how long your novel is planned to be."

"That's … amazing!" Goldilocks said. "You're a genius, Baby Bear."

Baby Bear looked modestly at the floor. "The nice thing about a spreadsheet is that you can also put in other columns to help you plan your scenes and track progress. You might record how long it took you to write the scene. Or how many words you actu-ally wrote in the scene. And if you have a carefully plotted story where the timing matters very much, like a bank robbery or a murder mystery, you might need a column with time stamps."

"What's a time stamp?" asked Mrs. Hubbard.

"It's the exact time at which the scene happened. When minutes are important and you want to make sure that your timeline is realistic and plausible, you can put the time stamp for each scene in a time stamp column. Mystery writers often need a timeline in their novels to keep everything straight."

Goldilocks felt her heart start racing. She leaped off of the hot seat and grabbed her purse and went running out of the room.

"Goldilocks, come back!" Baby Bear shouted after her.

But Goldilocks kept running.

Baby Bear had given her an idea.

There might possibly be a way to prove whether the Big Bad Wolf was lying or telling the truth.

Chapter Fifteen

GOAL, CONFLICT, SETBACK

Goldilocks raced down the hallway, fumbling with her conference schedule. She scanned the day's classes and found what she was looking for. Papa Bear was teaching a workshop on fairy tales in classroom 102B.

She burst into the room, breathing hard, her face feeling very flushed.

Papa Bear scowled at her. "Miss Goldilocks, what is the meaning—"

"Your cell phone!" she said. "Does it show a time stamp of when you called the police yesterday?"

"I'm sure it does, but—"

"Please, I need to see it!" she said. "I think it might prove the Big Bad Wolf is innocent."

Papa Bear shook his head. "He's not innocent. I performed the citizen's arrest myself. He was washing his hands—probably getting the blood off."

"Did you see any blood in the sink?"

Papa Bear thought for a moment. "No ..."

"Did you see any blood on his fur?"

A long pause. "No ..."

"Please, can you just show me on your phone what time you called the police?"

Papa Bear sighed. "You're a very persistent young woman." He pulled out his phone and pecked at the screen for several seconds. "Here it is. I made the call at exactly 9:43 a.m. But I don't see what good that does you."

"It gives us a time stamp," Goldilocks said. "If it's before the murder of Little Pig ..."

Papa Bear just looked at her.

Goldilocks suddenly realized that she wasn't thinking straight. Papa Bear had arrested the Big Bad Wolf *after* he found Little Pig dead. A time stamp after the murder was no use. She shook her head. "I'm sorry. I must be very stupid. I just thought ..."

A young woman in Papa Bear's class began whispering to the older woman next to her. They both smirked and gawked at Goldilocks.

Goldilocks wanted to die of embarrassment. But that wouldn't help the Big Bad Wolf. She had to keep trying. "Please, can you tell me exactly what time you found Little Pig dead in the coffee shop?"

Papa Bear's huge bushy eyebrows knitted together. Finally, he began fishing in his wallet. "It won't do you any good, but I have my receipt for the coffee I bought just before I found Little Pig. It's a business expense, and ... yes, here it is."

Goldilocks inspected the receipt closely. "You bought the coffee at 9:35 a.m. That was eight minutes before you caught the Big Bad Wolf in the men's room. What did you do after you bought the coffee?"

Papa Bear shrugged. "I went straight out the side door into the back patio and saw Little Pig lying there in a pool of blood. I ran back inside the coffee shop and told the barista to call an ambulance. Then I ran back outside and checked Little Pig for any signs of life. He was clearly dead. There were some wolf prints in the dirt right nearby. I came out of the back patio through that arch in the hedge and looked in all directions for signs of the killer. There was nobody in the parking lot. I went back to the patio and asked myself where I would go if my paws were bloody."

"Did you see any other tracks?" Goldilocks said.

Papa Bear shook his head. "Just Little Pig's own hoofprints in a small muddy patch beside his body. But I had a hunch, so I went into the main building and checked the men's room. And there was the Big Bad Wolf, washing his paws. I performed a citizen's arrest and called the police."

"So all of that happened in a span of eight minutes," said Goldilocks. "And Little Pig was already dead at 9:35, when you bought the coffee?"

"I'm sure," said Papa Bear. "I took the coffee straight to the patio, and there he was."

Goldilocks nodded. It wasn't enough information, but it was something.

Papa Bear looked at his watch.

Goldilocks took the hint and said "Thank you," and backed out into the hallway. She felt horribly discouraged. The idea of time stamps had made a lot of sense when Baby Bear said it, but now she couldn't see that it had got her anywhere.

"Everything okay?" Robin Hood called from down the hall.

Goldilocks shook her head. She didn't know what to do next. She had promised the Big Bad Wolf she would help, but so far, she hadn't done a thing except make a fool of herself.

"Want to go get some coffee?" Robin Hood said when she reached him. "Because you are, like, one amazing wench, and—"

"Leave me alone!" Goldilocks shouted. "And stop calling me a wench. Nobody calls women wenches anymore. It's rude and disrespectful."

Robin Hood looked shocked. "Really? I'm sorry—"

"Don't be sorry. Just … grow up." Goldilocks walked past Robin Hood as fast as she could. She strode down the hall, past the main auditorium, past Baby Bear's classroom.

Down at the end of the hall was a sign that said "Conference Director."

Goldilocks didn't know what the director could tell her, but it would be worth trying. She opened the door and stepped in.

The office was empty. It was a small room with three large gray metal office desks against the far wall. Several computers hummed on the desks.

And in the middle of the third desk was an expensive digital camera.

Goldilocks felt her heart double-thump.

She picked up the camera and studied it.

Then she heard voices from the next office, which connected to this one through a doorway.

Terrified, Goldilocks ran out of the office, stuffing the camera into her purse.

The hallway was empty, but she heard voices behind her in the director's office.

Goldilocks ran.

She ran all the way back down the long hall and out into the bright morning sunlight.

She kept running until she reached the coffee shop. Somebody was inside, so she ducked around to the back patio and sat under the shade of a large umbrella in the far corner and laid her purse carefully on the table. She looked all around. It was quiet and secluded here. The tall hedge protected her from the view of people in the conference center.

Goldilocks took out the camera and turned it on and began scrolling through the images.

The most recent were pictures of the Big Bad Wolf being pushed into the police car. Then pictures of Papa Bear. Pictures of Mama Bear and Baby Bear watching the police. There were several pictures of herself.

Goldilocks frowned. Her hair looked horribly windblown. She really needed to do something—

"What have you got there?" said a voice.

Goldilocks looked up, and nearly fainted.

A young pig stood there—looking very much like Little Pig, only smaller. He was wearing a high-quality sport jacket, but no tie or pants or anything else.

"Oh!" Goldilocks said. "Who are y-you?"

"I'm Tiny Pig. My uncle was murdered here yesterday. I flew in this morning to get some answers."

"I'm so sorry about your loss," Goldilocks said. "Your uncle was in my writing class, so I knew him just a little bit. I'm looking for answers too, and I'm hoping that I've found them."

Tiny Pig's eyebrows leaped up. "R-really? What have you learned?"

Goldilocks held up the camera. "I ... um, borrowed this from the conference photographer. He took some pictures yesterday, and I think ... well, I'm hoping there are some clues here."

"May I join you?" Tiny Pig's jowls were quivering. "My uncle was my only living relative. We were very close."

Goldilocks pulled up a chair next to hers. "Have a seat and we can look together."

Tiny Pig sat next to her. His whole body seemed to be rippling with nervous energy.

Goldilocks could only imagine how awful he felt. She continued scrolling through the images. There were shots of the police cars after they had arrived.

The next shot was in Baby Bear's classroom, with Goldilocks and Baby Bear looking at each other wearing fake smiles.

Goldilocks felt her breath coming in little gasps. She scrolled rapidly, looking, looking ...

There!

The photographer had taken one shot that showed most of the room.

Clearly visible in the far corner was the Big Bad Wolf, fast asleep.

"The time stamp for this is 9:39!" said Goldilocks. "That proves it!"

Tiny Pig peered at the screen. "Proves what?"

"This was taken four minutes after Papa Bear found your uncle dead," Goldilocks said. "This proves the Big Bad Wolf didn't murder him. This is wonderful news!"

Tiny Pig jumped up. "Oh, my word!" He pressed his right front hoof to his heart. His face had gone pale and damp. "The Big Bad Wolf … not the murderer?"

"Exactly! We've discovered the proof!" Goldilocks said. "We've got to tell the conference director. This means the murderer is still out and about somewhere. We might be in danger. Especially you."

Tiny Pig's jowls were working, and he seemed to be having trouble breathing. "Oh, my word! Miss, I feel faint. Can you help me?"

"I'll call an ambulance." Goldilocks reached for her purse to get her phone.

"Don't you dare!" Tiny Pig pulled a small syringe out of the breast pocket of his jacket and pointed it straight at her.

Chapter Sixteen

REACTION, DILEMMA, DECISION

*G*oldilocks leaped up, holding her purse in front of her as if it were a shield. Her heart was beating so fast it hurt. Adrenaline raced through her body. Her breath was coming in short little gasps, and her entire body felt horribly cold. She wanted to run, but her feet felt frozen in place. She looked frantically for a way to get past Tiny Pig to the arch that led out of the court.

Tiny Pig adjusted his position to block her path and then took a step toward her, the needle of the syringe pointed directly at her. "This won't hurt a bit, Miss." He took another step.

Goldilocks saw that she was trapped in the corner of the patio. She backed up and backed up, trying desperately to catch her breath. She wanted to scream, but she couldn't say a word.

Tiny Pig moved closer.

Goldilocks tried to dial 911, but the phone fell out of her nerveless hand.

Closer.

Goldilocks clutched her purse, thinking she was going to faint at any moment.

Closer.

Goldilocks reached in her purse and grabbed her canister of pepper spray. Her fingers felt as big and clumsy as sausages.

Tiny Pig rushed at her.

Goldilocks squeezed.

A thin spray of pepper hit Tiny Pig in the eyes.

He collapsed on the ground, squealing in rage, pawing at his eyes.

Suddenly, Goldilocks could breathe again. She sucked in air and screamed as loud as she could.

Tiny Pig wiped his eyes. Incredibly, he was still holding the syringe. He began crawling toward her, half-blind.

Goldilocks screamed again.

Robin Hood appeared through the arch in the hedge. "Sounds like a wench in distress—"

"*He's* the murderer!" Goldilocks pointed at Tiny Pig. "Do something!"

Tiny Pig pushed himself closer to her, jabbing the syringe blindly at her legs.

Robin Hood whipped out an arrow and nocked it in his bowstring. "Freeze, pig!" he shouted. "If you move a muscle, you'll be roasting in Sherwood Forest over an open fire tonight."

Tiny Pig froze.

Goldilocks stepped past Tiny Pig and picked up her phone and dialed 911.

It rang twice and then ...

A voice said, "What is the nature of your emergency?"

"I ... I need the police to come," Goldilocks said. "I think I've caught the real murderer of Little Pig."

Chapter Seventeen

PLANNING YOUR SCENES

The morning passed in a blur. The police came and arrested Tiny Pig. Goldilocks drove to the jail and waited for the Big Bad Wolf to be released. There was a long delay, but the police finally let him out. She brought him back to the conference center just in time for lunch. The entire conference burst into applause when Goldilocks and the Big Bad Wolf entered the cafeteria.

After lunch, they walked to the final session that Baby Bear would be teaching on the Snowflake Method. On the way, the Big Bad Wolf got a phone call.

Goldilocks couldn't hear what the caller was saying, but the Big Bad Wolf kept saying, "Yes, that's wonderful," and his smile kept getting wider and wider. He hung up just as they reached the classroom.

"What was that all about?" Goldilocks said.

The Big Bad Wolf's eyes gleamed with joy. "Tiny Pig confessed. And not only—"

"That's wonderful!" Goldilocks began shrieking in delight and threw her arms around him and gave him a gigantic hug.

Baby Bear opened the door. "Come in, both of you! Congratulations, Wolf. And congratulations, Goldilocks. You showed a lot of guts this morning. When everybody else had given up on the Big Bad Wolf, you followed your instincts."

"One amazing wench," Robin Hood said.

Goldilocks felt too happy to get angry about being called a wench.

The Big Bad Wolf wore a grin a mile wide. "You've restored my faith in humans," he said.

"I just … had a hunch," Goldilocks said. "When Baby Bear talked about time stamps, I realized that I might be able to find some evidence."

"But … dearie, why were you looking for evidence in the first place?" said Mrs. Hubbard. "The police don't often make mistakes."

"Ha!" said Robin Hood. "The Sheriff of Nottingham does nothing but make mistakes."

"I just …" Goldilocks felt very foolish. "I felt in my heart that the Big Bad Wolf wasn't the type to kill Little Pig."

The Big Bad Wolf hung his head modestly. "Thank you for believing in me. I just heard from my lawyer. As it turns out, Tiny Pig had a very good motive for killing his uncle. He was a trust-fund brat. When he came of age, he received all the money he inherited from his father—Little Pig's brother. But now he's spent just about all of it."

"So he wanted more from Little Pig?" Baby Bear said.

The Big Bad Wolf shook his head. "He wanted money, yes, so he called Little Pig two weeks ago to demand a cushy job. But Little Pig turned him down flat, and said something that got Tiny Pig thinking. Tiny Pig did some research, and that's when he decided that he wanted something money can't buy."

Goldilocks saw it all in a flash. "You didn't murder Little Pig's brothers. Which means somebody else did. Somebody who would benefit from them being gone. And Tiny Pig figured out who it was and how he did it."

"Little Pig!" shouted Robin Hood.

"Exactly," said the Big Bad Wolf. "As part of his business empire, Little Pig was the CEO of a drug company. Tiny Pig's syringe contained a powerful sedative—enough to kill you, Goldilocks. Enough to knock out Little Pig so he could be murdered in a way that looked like a wolf did it."

"Would it put a wolf to sleep for twenty-four hours so he wouldn't have an alibi on the day he was being framed for murder?" said Goldilocks.

The Big Bad Wolf's face lit up in an enormous smile. "My lawyer says Tiny Pig has proof that Little Pig did exactly that. As part of his plea bargain, Tiny Pig is giving that evidence to the police. My lawyer says I'll get my conviction overturned and my honor restored. It's all thanks to you, Blondie."

Baby Bear was jumping up and down with excitement. "Wolf, are you going to take on Goldilocks as your client?"

The Big Bad Wolf thought about that for a long minute. "I'd like to. We've become friends, and that's important to me, because I only work with people I like. But I also only work with excellent writers, so I'll need to see a polished draft of her book before I make a decision. Writing is a business, and even my friends don't get a pass."

Goldilocks felt so happy she wanted to scream. "I … I'd expect you to make decisions only if they're good business. I wouldn't want to work with an agent who makes decisions based on emotion. I don't have my novel written yet, but … I will."

"Are you ready to start writing?" Baby Bear said.

"I … sort of." Goldilocks wanted so badly to say yes. But the truth was that she wasn't quite there. She knew vaguely what would happen in her first scene. But she didn't know if it would be a good scene. She felt like she was still missing something.

Baby Bear was studying her intently. "You seem a little hesitant. Perhaps we should talk about step 9 in the Snowflake Method. It's about planning each scene before you write it."

Goldilocks felt a rush of excitement. "What's step 9?"

Baby Bear pointed to the hot seat. "We'll learn this best by doing it."

Goldilocks sat down.

Robin Hood whipped out his phone and took a picture of her. He looked at it and then handed it to her. "You are for sure one amazing wench, but you might want to think about finding a comb or something."

Goldilocks stared at the picture. Her hair was a hot mess. There was a smudge of mud on her cheek. The collar of her blouse had a streak of blood on it.

And she didn't care.

She handed the phone back to Robin Hood. "That's not important. What's important is how well you write, not what you look like. Baby Bear, tell me about step 9."

"Bravo," said the Big Bad Wolf, who was standing off to the side, beaming. "Blondie, I'm beginning to think you have a little wolf blood in you."

"Before you write any scene, you may find it helpful to plan it," Baby Bear said. "There are two standard patterns for a scene. One pattern is called a Proactive Scene, which starts with a goal, continues for most of the scene with conflict, and then ends with a setback."

The Big Bad Wolf stepped to the whiteboard and wrote:

PARTS OF A PROACTIVE SCENE:
   1) Goal
   2) Conflict
   3) Setback

Baby Bear continued. "The other pattern is called a Reactive Scene. It starts with an emotive reaction to the setback in the previous scene. Then most of the scene is spent in analyzing the dilemma of what to do next. The scene ends with a decision."

The Big Bad Wolf wrote:

PARTS OF A REACTIVE SCENE:
    1) Reaction
    2) Dilemma
    3) Decision

"Dearie, I'm getting lost," said Mrs. Hubbard. "Can you give us some examples?"

Baby Bear thought for a minute. "This morning when Goldilocks went running out of here, why did she do that?"

"Dude, she wanted to find some time stamps for before and after the murder of Little Pig," said Robin Hood.

Goldilocks nodded. "My goal was to get time stamps."

Baby Bear grinned. "A very modest goal, but also achievable. It was a steppingstone on the way to her larger goal, which was to clear the Big Bad Wolf's name. But it turned out to be a fairly difficult goal, right?"

"It was horrible," Goldilocks said. "I asked Papa Bear for help, and he didn't want to be bothered, so I pestered him until he let me see the time stamp from his phone. But then it wasn't any use."

"Ah, you ran into conflict, and then you gave up and cried," said Baby Bear. "Is that right?"

"I did not!" Goldilocks said hotly. "Then I asked Papa Bear for his coffee receipt, and he found it, and that was the first part of the evidence I needed."

"But then you had no idea what to do next," said Baby Bear. "More conflict. So then you cried, am I right?"

"Dude, you are, like, obsessed about this crying thing," Robin Hood said. "And you are way wrong. She ran into me and yelled my ear off, and then she went stomping off like a wench on the warpath. She was awesome."

"Then what happened?" Baby Bear said.

"I ... um, found that photographer's camera in the conference director's office. But I heard voices coming—"

"More conflict," said Baby Bear.

"And I borrowed the camera and ran and hid in the coffee shop patio. And then Tiny Pig showed up, and we found the proof that the Big Bad Wolf didn't murder Little Pig."

"Dude!" Robin Hood crowed at Baby Bear. "That's not a setback. Hate to burst your bubble, but that is, like, one awesome victory. Goldilocks found the time stamp she was looking for. She achieved her goal. You better rethink your little theory there."

Goldilocks started shaking. "But then Tiny Pig pulled out his syringe and tried to kill me."

"Setback," said Baby Bear with a smug little smile.

"Goal-conflict-setback." The Big Bad Wolf checked each one off on the whiteboard. "I think the technical term here is 'bazinga.'"

"And then I came in and saved the day," said Robin Hood.

"You're jumping the gun," said Baby Bear. "There's more that happened before you came in. We've just now worked through a complete Proactive Scene, but that's not the end of the story. What happened next, Goldilocks? What did you do?"

Goldilocks remembered how she'd been frozen in place for a few seconds. "I ... I didn't *do* anything. I was so scared, I couldn't move, couldn't think, couldn't even scream. I guess I'm just a dumb blonde."

The Big Bad Wolf came up behind her and started kneading her shoulders. "You did exactly what most humans do the first time they face combat. People talk about 'fight or flight,' as if those are the only two options. But there's a third option—freeze. It's 'fight or flight or fright.' What you did was natural, and nothing to be ashamed of. At least you didn't stay frozen, like some humans would have. And the reason is because you've been learning how to do courageous things lately. When the pinch came at the end, you had some courage in your emotional reserves."

"The point is that your first action was not an *action* at all," said Baby Bear. "It was a *reaction*. An emotive response to the very dangerous setback in the previous scene. Bears, pigs, wolves, humans—all of us feel emotions. Fear, joy, anxiety, love, rage. We can't help ourselves. We're not robots. We feel."

"Well, it was horrible," Goldilocks said. "I looked to see if I could get past Tiny Pig."

"You were in a dilemma, so you considered your first option," said Baby Bear.

"But he moved to block me, and I saw he had me cornered. So then I backed away from him."

"Your first option failed, so you tried a second one."

"And I backed right into the corner and couldn't go any further. So I tried to use my phone."

"Your second option failed, and you tried a third."

"But I dropped my phone, and then I remembered my pepper spray."

"Your third option failed, and you thought of a fourth."

"I knew that would work, so I—"

"Decision!" Baby Bear said. "After considering three options that didn't work, you made a decision on the fourth."

"Would you just let me finish?" Goldilocks said. "So I reached into my purse and grabbed my pepper spray and let him have it right in the eyes."

"That decision marks the end of a very short Reactive Scene," said Baby Bear. "It also became the goal for the next Proactive Scene, which began immediately."

Goldilocks saw it. "So you're telling me that Proactive and Reactive Scenes just kind of chain together like that?"

"Exactly," said Baby Bear. "Now let's think about the first scene of your novel. Dirk parachutes into Elise's garden and breaks his leg. What's the goal of this scene?"

"To parachute into France behind enemy lines and hole up for the night."

"And that goes smoothly, does it?"

Goldilocks shook her head. "No, there's anti-aircraft fire, which they dodge. There's a German plane that chases them and shoots them up. The engine catches fire. Dirk jumps out, but the other commandos are all killed when the plane explodes."

"That's the conflict," Baby Bear said. "Enough for a scene of a few pages, very exciting. And then at the end, Dirk achieves his goal?"

"No! He breaks his leg and passes out," Goldilocks said.

"Dude! That's what I'd call a setback," Robin Hood said. "Hey, this little theory thing of yours actually works."

"Shocking," said Baby Bear. "That's your first scene, Goldilocks. Can you write that scene now?"

"I can if I make a few notes." Goldilocks opened a new document on her laptop and rapidly typed one sentence for her goal, one for her conflict, and one for her setback. "Wow! That was easy. Can we do the next scene?"

"What's going to happen next?" Baby Bear said.

"Elise hears something, so she goes outside and finds Dirk."

"So Elise is your point-of-view character, right?"

Goldilocks nodded and typed "Elise."

"What does she feel right away when she hears the noise?"

"Um … curious. A little nervous. Maybe worried that Monique is having a nightmare."

"That's not much of a reaction," Baby Bear said. "Perhaps this shouldn't be a Reactive Scene."

Goldilocks felt horrible. "Oh, my! Is something wrong with my story?"

Baby Bear shook his head. "Not all emotive reactions are worth a full Reactive Scene. Most professional novelists write many more Proactive Scenes than Reactive Scenes. Let's assume we can skip the Reactive Scene and go straight to a Proactive Scene. What's her goal?"

"To find out what that noise was."

"Good. Type that up," said Baby Bear.

Goldilocks did. "So her conflict is that she checks on Monique, and she's fine. She goes out in front to see if a tree fell, and everything's fine. She goes out in the back and … there's a man lying in her garden! And he's muttering something in English."

"There's your setback," said Baby Bear. "Then what does Elise feel?"

"She's terrified," Goldilocks said. "She sees right away that he's an American commando. She knows that she has to turn him in to the authorities, because she'll be shot if she's discovered harboring an enemy of the Nazis."

Baby Bear just looked at her. "But …?"

"But she can't! He would be killed. He's trying to liberate her country. How could she turn him in? And …" Goldilocks blushed. "He's very handsome. Is it shallow of Elise to notice that he's handsome, so she wants to save him?"

The Big Bad Wolf howled with delight. "Blondie, there's nothing to be ashamed of there. You humans act like your mating instincts are unnatural or something. Elise isn't being shallow when she notices Dirk is handsome. She's going deep there—deep into her wolf brain."

Mrs. Hubbard scowled at him. "Wolf brain, my eye! Young man, if you're going to spout your nonsense evolutionary theories that have been disproven—"

"Peace!" Baby Bear said. "Let's stay focused, everyone. Elise has a dilemma. Turning in Dirk would violate every instinct of human decency, patriotism, and physical attraction that Elise has. But harboring Dirk would violate her instinct for survival *and* her instinct to protect her cub. Um, her daughter."

Goldilocks was typing furiously. "And her decision—she's got to decide to take care of him and hide him, but how can she do that when it's so dangerous?"

"What are Elise's Values?" Baby Bear said. "She has several Values—things she believes are more important than anything else. But those Values are in conflict. They can't all be the most important thing to her. She must make a decision on which of her Values is truly most important. That's what decisions do—they expose our true beliefs."

"Nothing is more important than compassion," Goldilocks said. "That's her Value. It's true that Elise is afraid to die and afraid to endanger Monique, but she's more afraid to become like Henri —collaborating with the Nazis to hurt good people."

Baby Bear smiled. "I think you've got a couple of scenes fleshed out there, a short Proactive Scene and then a Reactive Scene, both from Elise's point of view."

Goldilocks read through what she'd typed. It was very rough. There was a lot more that she could say. But it was enough.

"I hate to be the dude with the bad news," Robin Hood said, "but we have, like, five minutes left in this class, and isn't there another step to cover in your Snowflake Method? Tough luck, bro bear, but you aren't gonna make it."

Goldilocks looked at the clock.

Robin Hood was wrong. There were only *three* minutes left before the class was due to end. She had hogged all the time, and now Baby Bear was not going to be able to finish his workshop.

Chapter Eighteen

WRITING YOUR NOVEL

*B*aby Bear grinned at the class. "It's time now for the tenth step of the Snowflake Method. This is the one that will take the most time to do, but it's the quickest to explain."

He went to the whiteboard and wrote:

STEP 10 OF THE SNOWFLAKE
1) Write the first scene of your novel.
2) Don't stop writing scenes until you're done.

He spun around and faced the class. "If you've done step 8, then you have a complete list of scenes for your novel. If you've done step 9, then you've planned each scene and you know in advance that it will move your story forward because it's either a Proactive Scene or a Reactive Scene. You are now ready to write your novel. So go do it."

He took a small bow.

The minute hand on the clock ticked over to the top of the hour.

The bell rang outside in the hallway.

The class erupted into cheers.

Goldilocks hurried to Baby Bear and wrapped him up in a giant hug. She hugged the Big Bad Wolf. She hugged Mrs. Hubbard. She even hugged Robin Hood, even though he smelled like a gallon of ale.

"Awesome wench," he said. "I mean chick! Not wench, chick."

Everybody was talking at once.

The Big Bad Wolf clapped a furry paw on Goldilocks's shoulder. "Well, Blondie, the ball is in your court. You're a different woman than the one who walked in here a few days ago. Are you ready to write your novel?"

"I'm totally ready," Goldilocks said. "I can't wait."

*T*hat evening, after the children were in bed, Goldilocks sat down at her computer and opened her novel in her word processor and looked at what she'd written so far. There was only one word typed. "The."

Goldilocks deleted it.

And began typing madly.

*D*irk Steele gripped the hard metal seat with one hand and tightened the straps of his chute with the other. The plane was bucking and jumping like a rodeo bull. "How much farther to the drop zone?"

The jumpmaster finished vomiting into a small paper bag. "About five minutes, if—"

Another anti-aircraft round exploded outside, so close it felt like a hammer had smashed Dirk directly on the eardrum.

The rear gunner cursed. "And now we've got Jerry on our tail!"

The plane dove toward the earth, jerking and jinking wildly.

The sound of a machine gun clattered behind them.

"Almost there!" screamed the pilot. "Prepare for—"

Something slammed into the right wing.

A horrific explosion shook the entire plane.

"Out now!" The jumpmaster staggered to the side door and flung it open. "Dirk, get out—now, now, now!"

Dirk dove through the door, praying that his chute would do its duty.

The freezing airstream slammed him with a giant fist, spinning him like a top.

A German fighter plane sped by, machine guns blazing.

A flash like lightning.

An explosion like thunder.

A shock wave like a cement truck.

For a few seconds, Dirk couldn't breathe.

He opened his eyes and looked back to see who else had made it out of the plane.

The last thing he saw before he dropped into the clouds was ...

Nothing.

Fear hit Dirk like a hammer.

The plane was gone.

The night sky was empty.

The other nine commandos, the jumpmaster, the rear gunner, the pilot, the copilot—all dead.

He was alone, ten thousand feet above France, dropping like a rock toward a region teeming with half a million German soldiers.

Dirk felt for the duffel bag of explosives strapped to his chest. It would not be enough to take out the target.

The mission was one hour old, and already it had failed.

❄

$\mathcal{G}$oldilocks finished typing and looked at her watch. In eighteen minutes, she had written 314 words.

She jumped up and began dancing in a little circle. Baby Bear's Snowflake Method was just right.

Chapter Nineteen

SUMMARY OF THE SNOWFLAKE METHOD

*H*ere are the ten steps of the Snowflake Method.
The main purpose of these steps is to help you write your first draft. (When you're editing your story, you may also find these steps useful in helping you restructure your story and deepen your characters. But that's a secondary purpose.)

If you find that some of these steps aren't useful to you, then don't do them. You'll quickly learn which steps are most valuable to you. Focus on those. And if there are other steps that you find valuable, add them to your list. Your goal is to get a strong first draft. These steps are guidelines to get you there—they are not unbreakable rules.

After each step, you may want to revisit your earlier steps and revise your work. The earlier you make revisions, the better. The power of the Snowflake Method comes from helping you do many revisions early.

FIRST THINGS FIRST

Before you do any of these steps, you should know what category of novel you're writing and you should know who your target audience is. Your goal as a novelist is to delight your target audience.

Defining your target audience means deciding exactly what kind of story you want to write. Then your target audience is the set of people who would be delighted by that kind of story. You may be in your own target audience. If you aren't, it may help to visualize one typical person in that audience.

Answer these questions in writing:

My category is: _____

This is the kind of story I want to write: _____

This kind of story will delight my target audience because: _____

STEP 1: WRITE A ONE-SENTENCE SUMMARY

Give yourself one hour to write a single sentence that summarizes your novel. Make it less than twenty-five words if you possibly can. Focus on one or two characters and tell their story goal. Don't give away the ending.

The one-sentence summary is a marketing tool that you use to arouse curiosity. Shorter is better, because you want to memorize this sentence. Then, when somebody asks what your book is about, you can spiel it out without having to think.

The purpose of the one-sentence summary is to help people instantly know whether they are in your target audience.

If they are, then they'll say, "Tell me more!"

If they aren't, then they'll say, "My, look at the time!" and change the subject.

Your one-sentence summary also gives your fans a simple way to explain your book to their friends. So it's a key element of your word-of-mouth campaign.

STEP 2: WRITE A ONE-PARAGRAPH SUMMARY

Give yourself one hour to expand your one-sentence summary to a full paragraph of five sentences, organized like this:

1) Explain the setting and the story backdrop and introduce one or two lead characters.
2) Summarize Act 1, ending with your first disaster. This disaster forces your lead character to commit to the story.
3) Summarize the first half of Act 2, ending with your second disaster. This disaster causes your lead character to change his thinking from a false Moral Premise to a true one. As a result, your lead character commits to a new way of thinking and acting for the second half of the story.
4) Summarize the second half of Act 2, ending with your third disaster. This disaster causes your lead character (and your villain, if you have one) to commit to ending the story.
5) Summarize Act 3, in which you lead up to a final showdown where the lead character either succeeds or fails. You then resolve the story with a happy ending, sad ending, or bittersweet ending.

The purpose of the one-paragraph summary is to ensure that your story has a sound Three-Act Structure, with three strong disasters and a clear Moral Premise.

You will reveal your one-paragraph summary to your agent and editor, but *don't* reveal it to your potential readers! Your agent and editor need you to tell them how your story ends, but your readers want you to surprise them.

STEP 3: WRITE A SUMMARY SHEET FOR EACH CHARACTER

For each of your important characters, take up to an hour to produce a summary sheet that tells the essentials. Here are the things you need to know:

Role: (Hero, heroine, villain, mentor, sidekick, friend, etc.)

Name: The name of the character.

Goal: The concrete goal of the character for this story.

Ambition: The abstract ambition of the character.

Values: Several sentences that begin, "Nothing is more important than …"

Conflict: What keeps this character from achieving his goal?

Epiphany: What will this character learn by the end of the story?

One-sentence summary: A one-sentence summary of this character's personal story. (Your novel is the personal story of the lead character. All the other characters are the lead characters of their own personal stories.)

One-paragraph summary: A one-paragraph summary of the Three-Act Structure of this character's personal story.

You'll find that not all of these make sense for all your characters. Often, the villain has no epiphany. Some characters are too minor to need a one-sentence summary or a one-paragraph summary. Don't feel obligated to fill in everything for all characters.

STEP 4: WRITE A SHORT ONE-PAGE SYNOPSIS

Give yourself one hour to expand your one-paragraph summary into a full page. Do this by expanding each sentence in that paragraph to a full paragraph of its own.

If you go slightly over a page, that's fine. This one-page synopsis is solely for your benefit. You will never need to show it to anyone. Its purpose is to help you start filling in the details in your story.

People sometimes ask if the one-page synopsis should be single-spaced or double-spaced.

This synopsis is for your benefit, so make it single-spaced. That gives you about five hundred words, which is about right. If you want to double-space it for readability, then you'll probably go over a page, but nobody's going to be grading you for page count, so don't worry.

STEP 5: WRITE A CHARACTER SYNOPSIS FOR EACH CHARACTER

Give yourself an hour for each character and write up their back-story, along with their role in the main story. Usually, half a page to a page is about right. Explain why that character is the way they are, what they want out of life, and anything else that you find interesting. Explain how they fit into the story.

These character synopses are for your benefit. They help you to empathize with each character. Give special attention to the villain, since he usually gets shortchanged. Try to get inside his skin.

If you do a good job on these, you may someday put them in a proposal. Editors love these! Editors love great fiction, and great fiction is built on strong characters.

Very few writers ever put character synopses in their propos-als. This is a shame, because these are usually much more inter-esting than the plot synopsis, which is *required* in a proposal.

STEP 6: WRITE A LONG FOUR-PAGE SYNOPSIS

Give yourself two hours to expand your one-page synopsis into about four to five pages. Just take each paragraph from the one-page synopsis and expand it out to a page.

This four-page synopsis is for your benefit alone. You don't ever have to show it to anyone. Its purpose is to help you flesh out more details in your story.

People often ask how this is related to the synopsis that you must include with a proposal. That synopsis should be a bit shorter—generally two pages minimum and four pages maximum.

I recommend that you write your four-page synopsis first and then cut it down a bit to create your proposal synopsis. Yes, this takes more work, but each of these synopses has a special purpose.

STEP 7: WRITE A CHARACTER BIBLE FOR EACH CHARACTER

Take several hours per character and drill deep into them by creating a character bible for each one. This is where you will save all the details about your characters. Here are the sorts of things I usually include in my character bibles:

Physical information: Name, age, birthdate, height, weight, ethnic heritage, color of hair and eyes, physical description, and style of dressing.
Personality information: Sense of humor, personality type, religion, political party, hobbies, favorite music and books and movies, favorite color, and the contents of his wallet or her purse.
Environmental information: Description of home, education, work experience, family, best friend, male friends, female friends, and enemies.
Psychological information: Best and worst childhood memories, a one-line characterization, the strongest and weakest character traits, the character's paradox, their greatest hope and greatest fear, their philosophy of life, how the character sees himself, and how others see the character.

If you look online, there are many long lists of questions you can use to help you write your character bibles. None of these are perfect, but they give you examples of what should go into a character bible.

In the next chapter, you'll find the questions I used in creating the character bibles for Goldilocks and the other characters in this book.

You may find it helpful to find a picture of a real person who looks like each of your characters.

Here is your place to go deep. You want to know your character's family history, their religion, their politics, their philosophy, their personality type.

And of course, there are an endless number of superficial questions you can ask about each character. There are authors who insist that you should know each character's favorite ice cream. If that matters to you and your target audience, then write it down. If not, then don't.

STEP 8: WRITE A LIST OF ALL SCENES

Take a few days to create a list of every scene in your novel.

The scene is the fundamental unit of fiction. Each scene happens at a particular place and time and includes certain characters.

Each scene needs to have conflict. If there is no conflict in a scene, then it's not pulling its weight and you need to add conflict or kill the scene. Don't put in scenes that just "add atmosphere" or "explain the backstory" or "show the character's motivations." Conflict is the gasoline that makes a story run.

I recommend using a spreadsheet to write your scene list. Each row of the spreadsheet will represent one single scene.

You'll want one column to tell the point-of-view character of the scene. Another wide column will summarize what happens in the scene. You may add more columns with time stamps, projected word counts, or anything else. You are free to make your spreadsheets as complicated or simple as you like.

Some writers use 3x5 cards, with one scene per card. This works, but there are advantages to using a spreadsheet.

However you do it, make this list. It helps you see the story at a glance, and you can move scenes around as needed.

STEP 9: WRITE A PLAN FOR EACH SCENE

Take five minutes for each scene and jot down some crucial information that will help you write it. You may want to make a list of characters in the scene. You may want to describe the setting. If you have some amazing dialogue snippets for the scene, this is the place to save them.

I highly recommend that you analyze the scene's conflict. Is it a Proactive Scene or a Reactive Scene?

A Proactive Scene has this structure:
1) Goal
2) Conflict
3) Setback

A Reactive Scene has this structure:
1) Reaction
2) Dilemma
3) Decision

There is no standard length for a scene. A scene can be a hundred words or five thousand words. My own personal average for my suspense fiction is about a thousand words per scene, which is four manuscript pages. Faster-paced fiction has shorter scenes. Slower-paced fiction has longer scenes. Choose the scene length that works for you.

STEP 10: WRITE YOUR NOVEL

You now have a well-structured story planned. The story has a good hook. It has a sound Three-Act Structure. It has a number of deep, well-motivated characters. It has a complete list of scenes, and each scene has a strong conflict that will drive the story.

At this point, you are frothing at the mouth in your eagerness to write your novel.

Do so.

For each scene in your scene list, read everything you've planned for the scene and then just start typing.

For a Snowflaker, this is the joy of fiction—writing the first draft of a novel that you already know is going to be a great story.

CLOSING THOUGHTS

Remember that not everybody is a Snowflaker, and that's okay. Some people *must* write seat-of-the-pants. Some people *must* write a synopsis. Some people have other creative paradigms.

What matters is that you find a way that works well for you, so that you can write the first draft of your novel.

If the Snowflake Method works for you, then use it and be happy.

If only a few parts of it work for you, then use those and be happy.

If none of it works for you, then find some other method and be happy.

The Snowflake Method is nothing more nor less than the method that works best for me in writing fiction. If you can use it to guide your creativity as you write a powerful story, then I'll be thrilled.

I first posted my Snowflake article on my website in early 2003. In the years since, that page has been viewed more than 3.9 million times. I've heard from untold numbers of writers who've found it helpful. I would guess that there are tens of thousands of novelists around the world who use it.

I wish you the best of luck in your writing career, no matter what methods you use.

Have fun!

Randy Ingermanson ("the Snowflake Guy")
May 2014

P.S. If you find the Snowflake Method useful in writing your novel, I'd love to hear from you. Drop by my website at AdvancedFictionWriting.com and send me an email via my Contact page. It always makes my day to hear about your writing successes.

Chapter Twenty

THE SNOWFLAKE FOR THIS BOOK

I designed the story for this book using the Snowflake Method. In this chapter, I'll show you my design. You'll note that the Snowflake here is not quite in sync with the final story. That's fine. The point of the Snowflake Method is to get the book written. Your story will evolve as you write it. Don't feel bound to your design.

I created this chapter using my software Snowflake Pro and then exported it as a Word document. I tweaked the format to be suitable for a book and made a few changes in final editing. Because the story is so short, I skipped the long synopsis step, since that seemed to be overkill. It's important to adapt the Snowflake Method to the needs of your book.

BOOK INFO

Title: How To Write a Novel Using the Snowflake Method
Genre: Business Parable
Target Length: 40,000 words

Target Reader: A fiction writer who wants to write a novel and doesn't know how to get started.

AUTHOR INFO

Name: Randy Ingermanson

STEP 1: ONE-SENTENCE SUMMARY

A young woman has an impractical dream to write a novel, but she fears that other people won't like her writing.

STEP 2: ONE-PARAGRAPH SUMMARY

Goldilocks has always wanted to write a novel, but everyone in her family told her it was "impractical," so she put off her dream until her children started school. She begins taking classes at a writing conference, and Baby Bear invites her to try the Snowflake Method, but then he's gunned down in cold blood by the Big Bad Wolf. Goldilocks begins using the Snowflake Method, but when she creates a sympathetic villain, Little Pig tells her she's ruined her story. She goes to lunch with the Big Bad Wolf and soon realizes that he is a wonderful person with a tough exterior, and she really wants him to be her agent, but then he's arrested for the murder of Little Pig. Goldilocks finds the proof that he's innocent, and the real murderer tries to kill her, but she disables him with pepper spray and the Big Bad Wolf is freed.

STEP 3: CHARACTER SHEETS

Goldilocks
Role: Heroine/villain (she is her own worst enemy)
Values:

Nothing is more important than doing what you love.

Nothing is more important than making sure other people think well of you.

Nothing is more important than doing the right thing.

Ambition: To be a great novelist.

Goal: To write the first draft of her novel.

Conflict: She doesn't know how to get started because she's afraid that she's not a good novelist and she has a hard time worrying about what people will think of her.

Epiphany: She learns to trust her own instincts as a storyteller.

One-Sentence Summary: A young woman has an impractical dream to write a novel, but she fears that other people won't like her writing.

One-Paragraph Summary: Goldilocks has always wanted to write a novel, but everyone in her family told her it was "impractical," so she put off her dream until her children started school. She begins taking classes at a writing conference, and Baby Bear invites her to try the Snowflake Method, but then he's gunned down in cold blood by the Big Bad Wolf. Goldilocks begins using the Snowflake Method, but then when she creates a sympathetic villain, Little Pig tells her she's ruined her story. She goes to lunch with the Big Bad Wolf and soon realizes that he is a wonderful person who puts on a tough exterior, and she really wants him to be her agent, but then he's arrested for the murder of Little Pig. Goldilocks finds the proof that he's innocent, and the real murderer tries to kill her, but she disables him with pepper spray and the Big Bad Wolf is freed.

Baby Bear

Role: Mentor

Values:

Nothing is more important than the truth.

Nothing is more important than writing well.

Nothing is more important than fostering talent.

Ambition: To be the best fiction teacher in the world.

Goal: To teach Goldilocks how to plan her novel before she writes it.

Conflict: Goldilocks has irrational fears that she has no talent as a writer.

Epiphany: <No epiphany defined yet>

One-Sentence Summary: A young bear must teach a class of wannabe writers how to become professional novelists, but his most talented student has no confidence in her writing, and his agent friend keeps alienating people.

One-Paragraph Summary: Baby Bear invites his friend the Big Bad Wolf to help him out at a writing conference. Goldilocks is doing well, and it looks like she has talent, but she has a tiff with the Big Bad Wolf. Once that's resolved, Baby Bear pushes Goldilocks to improve her villain, but then Little Pig almost convinces her that she's all wrong. Just as Goldilocks is getting some confidence in herself, the Big Bad Wolf murders Little Pig, and Goldilocks takes up the lost cause of trying to prove he's innocent. But Goldilocks is right and the wolf is innocent, vindicating Baby Bear's judgment of both of them.

Big Bad Wolf

Role: Mentor

Values:

Nothing is more important than making something big out of your life.

Nothing is more important than being true to yourself.

Nothing is more important than the way of nonviolence.

Nothing is more important than honor.

Ambition: To be the world's greatest literary agent.

Goal: To find a new novelist he can turn into a superstar.

Conflict: Most novelists just don't want to work hard enough to excel at their craft.

Epiphany: <No epiphany defined yet>

One-Sentence Summary: A young and hungry wolf is searching for the writer of the Next Big Thing, but he's got a bad reputation and people are afraid of him.

One-Paragraph Summary: The Big Bad Wolf was framed for the murder of two pigs at the age of nineteen and sent to prison, where he was eventually paroled. Now he's a rising star literary agent and has come to the conference looking for talent, but his straight talk alienates Goldilocks. Little Pig is at the conference and is trying to make things difficult for the Big Bad Wolf. When Little Pig tries to lure away Goldilocks from her real calling, the Big Bad Wolf tells him off, and then is arrested an hour later when Little Pig is murdered. Goldilocks proves the Big Bad Wolf is innocent and he is freed.

Little Pig

Role: Antagonistic friend, murder victim in secondary storyline

Values:

Nothing is more important than money.

Nothing is more important than survival.

Nothing is more important than being famous.

Ambition: Become a famous novelist, if he doesn't have to work too hard.

Goal: Take a class in fiction writing and figure out the shortcuts to getting published, or else hire somebody to do the parts he doesn't like.

Conflict: Writing is harder than he had thought, and he really would rather pay somebody else to do the hard stuff.

Epiphany: <No epiphany defined yet>

One-Sentence Summary: A wealthy business-pig takes a course in fiction writing because he thinks it should be a piece of cake to write a best-selling novel.

One-Paragraph Summary: Little Pig has had a very successful career in business and is now looking to retire and write brilliant, stupendous fiction—a heartbreaking work of staggering genius.

When he learns that it's harder than it looks, he tries to find a coauthor, but nobody is interested. He then asks Goldilocks for her help, but the Big Bad Wolf intervenes and tells Little Pig off. Little Pig's nephew has been trying to get a job from him without success, and seeks him out at the conference. Tiny Pig murders Little Pig and frames the Big Bad Wolf, but is caught by Goldilocks when she proves that the Big Bad Wolf is innocent.

Tiny Pig
Role: Minor character, villain of secondary storyline
Values:
Nothing is more important than having a good time.
Nothing is more important than being wealthy.
Nothing is more important than having loads of friends.
Ambition: To be a wealthy and honored pig in the community without having to work hard.
Goal: To get a cushy job with his uncle, Little Pig, who runs a large corporation.
Conflict: Little Pig is about to retire and doesn't want to give Tiny Pig a job because he's lazy. Then Tiny learns that his uncle murdered his father.
Epiphany: <No epiphany defined yet>
One-Sentence Summary: A young, lazy pig tries to persuade his stuffy, rich uncle to give him a cushy job that won't require any work.
One-Paragraph Summary: Tiny Pig has had a successful college career getting drunk and chasing sorority girls, but his father is dead and his mother doesn't care about him and his trust fund has run out, and now he's going to have to sell off stock to stay afloat. Tiny Pig goes to his uncle and asks for a cushy job, but Little Pig is about to retire and, in any event, wouldn't give him a handout. Tiny Pig realizes that his uncle killed his father, and he knows that he stands to inherit everything, so he finds somebody to make up an injection that will paralyze his uncle so he

can be killed. Tiny Pig murders Little Pig and frames the Big Bad Wolf, but then finds that Goldilocks is trying to prove Wolf's innocence. Tiny has a backup injection and tries to kill Goldilocks, but she sprays him with pepper and Robin Hood arrests him.

Mother Hubbard
Role: Friend
Values:
Nothing is more important than having a full cupboard.
Nothing is more important than family.
Ambition: Maybe write a story someday and become rich.
Goal: Write a novel based on her personal experience with a bare cupboard.
Conflict: She just doesn't have much story.
Epiphany: She realizes that she doesn't want to be a novelist, she just wants to be rich.
One-Sentence Summary: An old woman decides to make a quick buck telling her personal experience as a poor widow in novel form.
One-Paragraph Summary: <No one-paragraph summary defined yet>

Robin Hood
Role: Friend
Values:
Nothing is more important than freedom.
Nothing is more important than tweaking the nose of the Sheriff of Nottingham.
Ambition: Live a life of adventure.
Goal: Write a story about his amazing life as an outlaw.
Conflict: He is pretty shallow and doesn't really want to work hard.
Epiphany: <No epiphany defined yet>

One-Sentence Summary: <No one-sentence summary defined yet>

One-Paragraph Summary: <No one-paragraph summary defined yet>

Papa Bear

Role: Minor character

Values: <No values defined yet>

Ambition: To teach his methods of fiction writing.

Goal: To teach how to outline a novel to young writers at a conference.

Conflict: <No conflict defined yet>

Epiphany: <No epiphany defined yet>

One-Sentence Summary: <No one-sentence summary defined yet>

One-Paragraph Summary: <No one-paragraph summary defined yet>

Mama Bear

Role: Minor character

Values: <No values defined yet>

Ambition: To teach her methods of fiction writing.

Goal: To teach how to write "organically" to young writers at a conference.

Conflict: <No conflict defined yet>

Epiphany: <No epiphany defined yet>

One-Sentence Summary: <No one-sentence summary defined yet>

One-Paragraph Summary: <No one-paragraph summary defined yet>

STEP 4: SHORT SYNOPSIS

Goldilocks has always wanted to write a novel, but everyone in her family told her it was "impractical," so she put off her dream until her children started school. When she decides to take classes at a writing conference, she first tries Papa Bear's outlining approach, but she finds it too hard for her. Then she tries Mama Bear's "organic" method, but she finds it too soft and squishy. Finally, she goes to Baby Bear's course on the Snowflake Method. It sounds good, but then Little Pig calculates that it will take forever to write her novel at the rate she's going. Goldilocks doesn't know what to think. She's wavering, and then the Big Bad Wolf walks into the classroom and guns down Baby Bear in cold blood.

Goldilocks is furious and attacks the Big Bad Wolf. Baby Bear jumps up and explains that he isn't dead, that it was just a stunt to show the importance of using disasters at the breakpoints between acts. Goldilocks sees how valuable the Three-Disaster Structure can be, and she whips out a one-paragraph summary that has the class breathless. However, when she begins doing her character sheets, she focuses on her hero and heroine and gives the villain short shrift. Little Pig wants to write an autobiographical novel and came to the conference to team up with an author who will do the hard work. Goldilocks produces an excellent one-page synopsis, and the Big Bad Wolf tells her she's showing some talent and invites her to lunch. In the next session, the wolf has disappeared, and Baby Bear asks to see Goldilocks's character synopses and tells her that her villain is two-dimensional. Goldilocks makes another try, and this time her villain is more believable, but Little Pig sneers that she's not going to impress the Big Bad Wolf with a villain like that.

Goldilocks goes to lunch, terrified of what the Big Bad Wolf will say. Will he sneer at her like Little Pig did? Will she lose her chance with the big-shot literary agent? But she decides that she must stop worrying what other people think. She talks to the Big Bad Wolf about her novel and then shows him her character synopses, and he starts crying. He tells her that it's hard to be the villain. People don't understand you and they think you're evil. He tells his story about how, as a young wolf, he was framed for the murder of two pigs. He served time in prison, and nobody ever believed he was innocent. Goldilocks sees that he has a soft and kind heart, and she desperately wants him to be her agent. After lunch, Goldilocks complains to Baby Bear that she now has to backtrack. He explains why that's normal and how the Snowflake Method encourages you to backtrack early, before you have a lot written. The next morning, Baby Bear teaches how to write a long synopsis. Little Pig pressures Goldilocks to help him with his story, and the Big Bad Wolf tells him off. Little Pig stalks out in a rage. Next, Baby Bear puts Goldilocks on the hot seat to help her develop her character bibles. The Big Bad Wolf has curled up in a back corner and gone to sleep. Baby Bear grills Goldilocks for quite a while, and a photographer comes in to take pictures. Nobody notices when the Big Bad Wolf leaves. But they all notice the wail of sirens in the background. Baby Bear goes to investigate and learns that Little Pig has been murdered. Only then does everyone see that the Big Bad Wolf is gone.

They all go out to see what's happened. The police have arrested the Big Bad Wolf, and Papa Bear is explaining how he discovered the body of Little Pig and then caught the Big Bad Wolf washing his hands in the men's room and arrested him and called the police. It's clear to everybody that the Big Bad Wolf is the murderer. Goldilocks visits him in jail, and he insists he's innocent—that he's been framed again. She believes him and spends the evening trying to figure out how to clear his name, but gets nowhere. She finally does her homework very late that night and staggers into class the next morning. Baby Bear teaches on the subject of scene lists, and he explains how to do one. When he mentions time stamps, Goldilocks gets very excited and goes rushing out. She finds Papa Bear and gets the receipt for his coffee. She finds the photographer's camera and steals it. She goes to a quiet spot in the coffee shop patio and looks at the pictures. Tiny Pig, the nephew of the murdered Little Pig, shows up and joins her. They find a photo of the Big Bad Wolf in class sleeping and the time stamp proves he is innocent. Tiny Pig pulls out a syringe and tries to inject Goldilocks. She sprays him with pepper, and Robin Hood arrives to help. Tiny Pig is arrested, Goldilocks is a hero, and the Big Bad Wolf is set free. That afternoon, Baby Bear gets Goldilocks to describe what happened. She tells about her Goal-Conflict-Setback and her Reaction-Dilemma-Decision. Baby Bear explains how those work and tells her she needs to sketch out her scenes in advance using those patterns. Once she's done that, she can start writing her novel. Goldilocks goes home and maps out scene 1 of her novel. Then she starts writing, and the words come very smoothly and easily. Goldilocks is very happy.

STEP 5: CHARACTER SYNOPSES

Goldilocks:

Goldilocks was a smart kid. She learned to read before she went to kindergarten, and she always had her nose in a book. When she was eight years old, she had a traumatic experience when she got lost on a walk in the woods. She came to the house of three bears and tasted their porridge, sat in their chairs, and slept in their beds. She escaped when the bears came home. Goldilocks put it all behind her, but the incident was traumatic enough that she developed an unhealthy fear of what other people think of her. So she has spent her life trying to make other people happy.

When Goldilocks started school, she loved writing stories. She won a writing contest in grade school and thought she might like to be an author someday. But when she started high school, her parents made it clear that they wanted her to do something serious when she grew up. They considered writing fiction a silly and childish pursuit, and told her that she needed to study something "practical" that would help her earn a living.

So Goldilocks studied marketing in college, and graduated with a degree that her parents thought was practical. She got a job and then soon got married. A year after getting married, she got pregnant with the first of two children, and she quit her job to focus on them. She had a daughter and son and spent several happy years with them. When the youngest started kindergarten, Goldilocks realized that she had now been out of the job force for nearly eight years and her skills were rusty. She could get an entry-level job at just above minimum wage. But the thought of doing more marketing for a company she didn't care about made her break out in hives. Her husband was earning a good income, and they didn't need the money. But she desperately wanted to do something useful with her life.

She decided to do something dreadfully impractical—she was going to write a novel like the ones she often read. But she quickly found that she had no idea how to get started. When she opened her word processor, the empty page stared at her and she had a terrible fear of getting started on the wrong track. She already felt like she was far behind, and she couldn't bear the thought of spending years of her life working on a manuscript that was unsaleable.

So she decided to go to a writing conference and see if she could quickly get up to speed on the task of writing a novel.

BABY BEAR:

Baby Bear is a young bear in his twenties who grew up in a home of writers. Both parents, Papa Bear and Mama Bear, are writers and teachers on the craft of fiction writing. Writing is in Baby Bear's blood.

Papa Bear is an outliner and Mama Bear is a seat-of-the-pantser. Neither of those approaches works for Baby Bear. He loves the Snowflake Method because it works for him.

He's now been teaching for a few years and is starting to get good as a teacher. At this conference, he wants to make a bit of a splash, but his first session isn't scheduled until late on the first day of the conference. He knows that people will go to hear Papa Bear and Mama Bear teach their methods first. He hopes that writers who find that these methods don't work for them may find the Snowflake Method better.

Baby Bear convinces a well-known literary agent, the Big Bad Wolf, to barge in on his class and fire a gun loaded with blanks at him. The purpose is to show his students what a disaster looks like. The stunt works better than he had expected, because it causes Goldilocks to get into a fight with the Big Bad Wolf.

Baby Bear sees a lot of potential in Goldilocks. On the surface, she looks like an airhead, but when he pushes her, she does the hard work of improving her one-sentence summary and her one-paragraph summary. When she begins work on her characters, it's clear that her hero and heroine are going to be fairly good, but her villain is a horrible two-dimensional caricature. Baby Bear wrestles with how to get her to do better, but no solution comes to mind.

When Goldilocks expands out her one-paragraph summary to a full page, it reads pretty well. Goldilocks doesn't like her villain very much, so she is not putting in the effort she needs on him. When she reads her character synopses, it's clear that the villain needs more work. Goldilocks makes a try at improving her villain, but Little Pig sneers that she's made him too soft and boring, and he claims that the Big Bad Wolf is going to hate her new villain. Goldilocks is wavering again. Baby Bear wants to tell her that she needs to focus on writing well, not on impressing agents or editors, but he realizes that she has to figure this out for herself.

After her lunch with the Big Bad Wolf, Goldilocks is showing new strength as a writer. She is no longer worried about what anyone thinks about her, and she is making good progress on her one-page synopsis and her character bibles. However, Little Pig is trying to hire a writer to help him, and he keeps bothering Goldilocks. The Big Bad Wolf tells him off, and Little Pig gets angry and stalks out.

Baby Bear puts Goldilocks on the hot seat and doesn't notice when the Big Bad Wolf leaves. But he does hear the sirens, and when he gets word that Little Pig has been murdered and the Big Bad Wolf has been arrested, he is very upset. He is responsible for the Big Bad Wolf coming to the conference, and now he's horrified that his kindness has turned into murder.

BIG BAD WOLF:

The Big Bad Wolf grew up in a rough neighborhood. As a juvenile, he saw his own uncle killed by a lynch mob who were angry at the murder of Little Red's grandmother. At the age of nineteen, he was framed for the murder of two pigs. All the Big Bad Wolf remembers is that he slept for a full day, and woke up the next day accused of murder. He had no explanation and no alibi, so he was convicted and served six years in prison.

He spent his time reading in the library and came out of prison determined to make something of himself. He worked in a literary agency for a couple of years and learned the industry and then hung up a shingle on his own and started taking clients. Authors were eager to sign on with him, because they figured he'd be a tough negotiator. And he was, because editors feared him.

The Big Bad Wolf wants to be the most successful agent in the business, and he's well on his way, but clouds are still hanging over him. There are people who won't ever forget that he did hard time in prison. For them, he's a dishonest scoundrel, a liar, a thief, and a murderer. And he can't see any way to live that down. One of the few people willing to give him a chance is Baby Bear, who likes him for his skill and literary judgment and sees past his rough edges.

When he meets Goldilocks, he's happy to see what a talented writer she is. She's got ideas and she's teachable. The only bad thing at the conference is that Little Pig is there, very full of himself and acting like he can buy his way to a position as a big-shot author, just because he's a wealthy tycoon. The Big Bad Wolf has words with Little Pig, and even threatens him with becoming lunch. This is stupid, and Big Bad Wolf knows it, but seeing Little Pig reminds him of the years he lost in prison.

The Big Bad Wolf has a nice dinner with Goldilocks and does his best to encourage her. She's making rapid progress, but he can't sell her work without a full proposal, which would include a longer synopsis. She'll also need some sample chapters, and preferably the full manuscript. The next day in class, the Big Bad Wolf takes a nap in the back corner. When he wakes up, Goldilocks is in the hot seat. The Big Bad Wolf tiptoes out to go to the men's room. While he's washing his hands, Papa Bear bursts in and accuses him of murdering Little Pig.

LITTLE PIG:

Little Pig is a wealthy business-pig who is ready to retire. He imagines that he could be a famous author, and it just seems reasonable that he ought to be able to buy his way into a book contract.

Little Pig grew up poor, but he started a business with his two brothers when they were young. The business grew and grew, but

Little Pig found his brothers annoying. They were lazy and old-fashioned, and they were holding back the company's growth. Little Pig felt certain that as long as they were in the company, it would never reach its potential. They were, in fact, robbing him of the success that was due him. He made an offer to buy them out, but they both refused.

So Little Pig made a sleeping potion, injected it into the Big Bad Wolf while he slept, murdered his brothers late at night in their houses, and left wolf prints all over. The Big Bad Wolf was arrested, and with no alibi, he was convicted. Now he's out of prison, but Little Pig knows that the wolf has no suspicions of him, so he's safe.

Little Pig comes to the conference with his idea for a novel. Papa Bear and Mama Bear are no help, so he goes to Baby Bear's classes. But Baby Bear keeps droning on about his Snowflake Method, which Little Pig finds very pedestrian. It sounds far too much like work. Why can't he just be creative and then hire out the details, as he always has in business?

But Baby Bear isn't having any of that, and the Big Bad Wolf keeps making fun of him. Little Pig gets more and more angry. The establishment is apparently stacked against him, and his money is no good for helping him get published. Finally, in a rage, he stalks out of class and goes to get a latte at the coffee shop. His nephew, Tiny Pig, texts him asking where he is. Tiny Pig was due to fly in tomorrow, but he's apparently in town already.

Little Pig tells him he's in the back patio of the coffee shop. Tiny Pig arrives and asks him about the job they had discussed a couple of weeks ago. Little Pig sneers and tells him he'd be better off going back to school and getting a real education instead of chasing sorority girls and getting drunk. Tiny Pig injects him with a paralyzing drug. Little Pig collapses to the ground, frozen. He watches while Tiny Pig makes wolf prints all around him and then slits his throat.

Little Pig's last thought as consciousness fades is that he's been hit by a speeding karma.

TINY PIG:

Tiny Pig is a trust fund brat. His father was murdered by the Big Bad Wolf and his mother is a socialite who has remarried and doesn't care much about him. Tiny Pig went to college and wasted all his time chasing sorority girls and getting drunk. Once he reached the age of twenty-one, he got full access to his trust fund and blew through the money incredibly fast. Now he's nearly broke, and thinks that the best thing to do is get a cushy job working for his uncle.

But his uncle, Little Pig, is about to retire. He refuses to help Tiny Pig get a job. Instead, he tells Tiny to go back to college and get a real education and then get an honest job and work his way up. But Little Pig lets slip some information about the death of Tiny's father. Tiny puts things together and realizes that Little Pig killed his father. He decides to kill his uncle, partly for revenge and partly so he can inherit his wealth.

Tiny gets a potion that paralyzes people and tracks down his uncle at the coffee shop. He injects him with the potion and puts wolf tracks all around him and then kills him.

His plan works. The Big Bad Wolf is arrested for the murder, and Tiny stands to inherit all of his money. But when Goldilocks finds proof that the Big Bad Wolf is innocent, Tiny has to act. He has an extra syringe, which he had made as a backup in case the first wasn't enough to disable his uncle. He tries to inject Goldilocks with the potion so he can kill her, but she sprays him with pepper. Robin Hood helps subdue him and Goldilocks calls the cops, and Tiny is hauled off to prison, where he soon confesses to his crime.

MOTHER HUBBARD:

Mother Hubbard is a poor widow who wants to get rich by writing a novel. She is fixated on what an interesting life she's had. But all that has ever happened to her is that she goes to her cupboard every day and it's bare.

Mother Hubbard is writing a novel about a poor widow exactly like herself. She does not want to write a romance, in which the widow finds a rich husband. She is not interested in writing a thriller or a mystery. She wants a slice-of-life story about herself.

Baby Bear is not much impressed with her story, and Mother Hubbard can't imagine why. She hates the arrogant and over-bearing Little Pig, and she's intimidated by the Big Bad Wolf. She does like Goldilocks, although the dear girl seems to live in a fantasy world.

ROBIN HOOD:

Robin Hood is a happy young man who lives in Sherwood Forest with his band of merry outlaws, feasting on poached deer and outwitting the Sheriff of Nottingham. He likes nothing more than a party that lasts all weekend, a huge barrel of ale, and swarms of willing wenches.

Robin Hood would like to write a novel, a series of episodes based on his own life. He's not a very hard worker, and when he goes to the writing conference to learn how it's done, he realizes that this is beyond his skill.

He can't help admiring Goldilocks. She's a hard worker and has a fascinating story. And she's quite a good-looking wench, although just a bit snooty. Robin Hood does not like Little Pig at all, and he finds the Big Bad Wolf a bit obnoxious.

When Little Pig is killed, Robin Hood isn't sad. When the Big Bad Wolf is arrested, Robin Hood isn't surprised. But when Goldilocks develops an unhealthy obsession to clear the Big Bad Wolf, Robin Hood is concerned. Wenches shouldn't take life so seriously. He tries to talk reason to her, but she gets angry at him and tells him that she doesn't like to be called a wench. Imagine that! She is one weird wench.

Robin Hood is not the kind of guy to let a wench get away without a pursuit, so he keeps an eye on her. When he sees her going to the coffee shop patio, he hangs out near the conference center, waiting for her to come back so he can talk to her. He sees Tiny Pig go to the back patio, but can't see or hear what goes on back there. But when he hears Goldilocks screaming for help, he's there in a flash, with an arrow nocked. He helps arrest Tiny Pig and hopes Goldilocks will thank him in the way any red-blooded guy wants to be thanked by a lovely wench.

STEP 6: LONG SYNOPSIS

This story was too short to need a long synopsis. The short synopsis was enough to allow me to create the scene list in step 8, so I skipped this step.

STEP 7: CHARACTER CHARTS

Goldilocks
Age: 30
Height: 5'5"
Weight: 115 pounds
Ethnic heritage: Northern European
Color of hair: Blonde
Color of eyes: Blue
Personality type: Amiable driver

Hobbies: Reading, writing

Favorite books: Goldilocks likes exciting thrillers with strong romantic storylines. She's a big fan of Ken Follett and Jack Higgins.

Favorite movies: Casablanca

Description of home: She lives in a three-bedroom house in the suburbs, about ten years old. She has a large kitchen with an island in the middle and marble counters.

Educational background: She went to college and got a degree in marketing.

Work experience: She worked for a year or two after college and before she had children, but she's been unemployed for about eight years and her job prospects are weak.

Family: She is married with a daughter in grade school and a son in kindergarten.

Worst childhood memory: She once got lost on a walk in the woods. When she came to a cabin, she went in and helped herself to some porridge. She broke some of the furniture and then fell asleep on a bed. When she woke up, three bears were in the house. She ran away, screaming, badly traumatized. Her parents were terribly disappointed in her and have told her all her life that she could have done better. She has an irrational fear of what other people will think.

Strongest character trait: Goldilocks is smart and energetic, and when she has things to do, she gets them done.

Weakest character trait: She's afraid of what other people will think of her, and this hamstrings her.

Greatest hope: To write a novel that everybody will love.

Deepest fear: To write a novel that everybody will hate.

How character sees self: She lacks self-confidence and doesn't realize how talented she actually is.

How others see character: They see her as smart and organized, with an endearing lack of self-confidence.

How character will change: Goldilocks will develop the self-confidence to trust her own instincts as a writer.

Baby Bear
Age: 29
Height: 3'2"
Weight: 200 pounds
Ethnic heritage: Bear
Color of eyes: Brown
Color of hair: Brown
Physical description: Baby Bear is a small bear.
Style of dressing: Wears fur
Sense of humor: Playful and a bit of a prankster
Personality type: Analytic amiable
Hobbies: Writing
Favorite books: A fan of the classic fairy tales. He reads widely in all categories, and likes suspense and fantasy and YA.
Favorite movies: Pride and Prejudice
Description of home: A small cottage in the woods, which he grew up in.
Educational background: He is smarter than your average bear, and got his degree in creative writing.
Work experience: Writes fiction and teaches fiction.
Family: The only son of Papa Bear and Mama Bear.
Male friends: His childhood friend is the Big Bad Wolf, who has a criminal record but seems to have reformed. However, the Big Bad Wolf still insists he didn't kill those pigs, and Baby Bear thinks he should just come clean. But he had an exemplary record in prison and is a good agent, and Baby Bear wants to give him a second chance.
Worst childhood memory: He went out for a walk one day as a cub and returned home to find his food eaten, his chair broken, and his bed slept in by a blonde human child who shrieked loudly

and ran away. Baby Bear has dreamed for years of finding the girl
and bringing her to justice.

Strongest character trait: Much smarter than your average bear.

Weakest character trait: Loyal to a fault. He grew up knowing the
Big Bad Wolf and has stood by him, even after he went to prison
and was clearly guilty.

Greatest hope: To be a great novelist himself someday, and not
just a famous teacher of fiction.

Deepest fear: That none of his students will ever be any good.

How character sees self: A smart bear who knows great fiction
and knows how to teach it.

How others see character: A great teacher and mentor.

Big Bad Wolf
Age: 29
Height: 6'0"
Weight: 180 pounds
Ethnic heritage: Wolf
Color of hair: Gray
Color of eyes: Black
Physical description: He is a huge wolf, with intense black eyes
that look right through you. He has gray fur and sharp canines
and he worked out a lot in prison, so he is incredibly well
muscled.
Style of dressing: Wears fur
Sense of humor: He has a sarcastic wit and doesn't hesitate to
puncture an inflated ego. However, he's quite kind to people who
lack self-esteem, and he'd never willingly hurt their feelings, but
he does sometimes just because he's a bit insensitive.
Personality type: Driver expressive
Hobbies: Long-distance running, reading, eating (he especially
likes pork ribs).
Favorite music: Punk rock

Favorite books: Thrillers, war novels, especially World War II novels, science fiction

Favorite movies: Die Hard (all four)

Favorite colors: Gray

Description of home: Has a nice, cozy cave.

Educational background: Self-taught while in prison. He read most of the prison library, and especially loves fiction.

Work experience: He was framed for the murder of two pigs at the age of nineteen and sent to prison. He worked in the laundry and was paroled for good behavior. He worked in a literary agency for two years and has recently started his own agency, the Big Bad Wolf Literary Agency.

Family: He comes from a pack of fiercely loyal wolves. However, none of them believe that he didn't kill the pigs, so he feels a bit uncomfortable with them. They're a violent bunch, and he's the quiet and studious one.

Male friends: He grew up with Baby Bear, who maintained friendship with him while in prison. However, Baby Bear has never quite believed that he's innocent. Baby Bear insists that Big Bad Wolf "had your reasons for what you did."

Female friends: Is dating a very nice she-wolf who has a booming career in real estate. Big Bad Wolf hopes something will come of it. Her family is a bit upset about his prison record, but she finds him brooding and mysterious and is probably more attracted to him because of his dangerous reputation than for his actual personality.

Enemies: Little Pig has always hated him for murdering his two brothers. It was Little Pig's weeping testimony on the witness stand that helped put Big Bad Wolf in prison.

Worst childhood memory: His favorite uncle was lynched by a mob of angry woodsmen after having lunch with Little Red's grandmother. Big Bad Wolf knows his uncle was guilty, but even so, he feels that the woodsmen were way out of line and should have waited for the court to exact justice. Big Bad Wolf despises lynch mobs.

One-line characterization: A dangerous-looking wolf with a soft heart.

Strongest character trait: Speaks impulsively and sometimes uses frightening language because he tends to exaggerate.

Weakest character trait: Tends to be too honest and forthright when giving his opinion, so he sometimes unknowingly hurts people's feelings.

Greatest hope: He wants to discover fresh new talent among the younger generation of writers.

Deepest fear: He fears that he will give in to the violent impulses of his wolfish nature.

How character sees self: A friendly, engaging, intelligent, but highly misunderstood wolf.

How others see character: A terrifying, sarcastic, unempathetic, dangerous wolf.

Little Pig
Age: 64
Height: 4'3"
Weight: 300 pounds
Ethnic heritage: Pig
Color of hair: Little Pig is bald.
Color of eyes: Pink
Physical description: He's a pig.
Style of dressing: No clothes. Sometimes wears a black bow tie.
Sense of humor: Little Pig is overly serious and never jokes.
Personality type: Driver analytic
Hobbies: He has an outstanding stamp collection, which he pays an assistant to keep up to date.
Favorite music: A big fan of Wagner
Favorite books: Any books on business management. How to Win Friends and Influence Enemies.

Favorite movies: Documentaries

Favorite colors: Pink

Description of home: Little Pig once had a fine brick home that he built himself. Later, as his business took off, he moved into a mansion in a gated community that has its own golf course. He doesn't use most of the rooms, but he has a few servants who live there and keep the place up—a butler, a cook, and a housekeeper.

Educational background: Harvard Business School

Work experience: Little Pig started a business selling straw, sticks, and bricks early in life with his brothers. Later, they moved into building supplies and created a chain of stores that competes with Home Depot and Lowe's, but targets contractors, not do-it-your-selfers. They then branched out into pharmaceuticals, where they made a killing. Little Pig became CEO after the tragic murder of his brothers.

Family: Little Pig's parents died many years ago, leaving him and his two brothers to fend for themselves. They began a business together, and it grew rapidly. After the tragic murder of Little Pig's brothers, the business grew exponentially under his leadership. Little Pig never married, but one of his brothers left a wife and a son (Tiny Pig). Tiny Pig grew up affluent and is a spoiled brat.

Best friend: Friends? Little Pig has no friends. But he has a lot of competitors.

Enemies: Little Pig's only enemies were his brothers, who were ruining the family business. So Little Pig killed them and inherited the stock of one of them and got full control of the company. His nephew Tiny Pig has now grown up and has a one-third share in the company, which earns him some dividends, but that's not enough for him. He wants a cushy job that will pay a high salary, and Little Pig knows he's incompetent, so he refuses to give him any sort of position in the company. Tiny is faced with having to sell off stock to maintain his lifestyle. But Tiny stands to inherit from Little Pig, and when he figures out that

Little Pig killed his father, he decides to kill two birds with one stone.

Best childhood memory: Little Pig loved to wallow in the mud on long summer afternoons with his brothers when he was a small child.

Worst childhood memory: Little Pig often heard terrifying tales as a child about the legendary Big Bad Wolf who huffed and puffed and blew down houses. Little Pig had nightmares about the Big Bad Wolf. When he finally met a wolf who was big and bad, it was an easy thing to use him as the fall guy for the murder of Little Pig's brothers.

One-line characterization: Little Pig is a male chauvinist pig, a psychopath who has got where he is by stepping on the hands of those below him on the ladder of success, and by pulling down those above.

Strongest character trait: Little Pig always gets what he wants, because he thinks that everybody has a price and everybody can be bought.

Weakest character trait: Little Pig lacks empathy and can't put himself inside the skin of anyone else. So he's completely unfit to be a novelist.

Greatest hope: Little Pig wants to be famous as a captain of industry and a great novelist—a multitalented but humble self-made pig.

Deepest fear: Little Pig is afraid that somebody will learn his deepest secret—that he killed his own brothers.

Philosophy of life: Take what you can! Give nothing back!

How character sees self: A self-made pig who pulled himself up by his own bootstraps and made a success from very humble beginnings.

How others see character: An arrogant, self-absorbed, egotistical pig who thinks he can buy everything and everyone.

How character will change: He'll be killed.

Tiny Pig
Age: 24
Height: 3'8"
Weight: 280 pounds
Ethnic heritage: Pig
Color of hair: Tiny is bald.
Color of eyes: Pink
Style of dressing: Pigs don't wear clothes. Tiny sometimes wears a nice sport jacket.
Sense of humor: He loves frat-boy humor. Nothing is funnier than dumping a pitcher of beer on your best buddy while he's getting friendly with his girlfriend on the couch.
Personality type: Expressive expressive
Hobbies: Drinking, playing pool, gambling, chasing girls
Favorite music: Hip-hop
Favorite books: Tiny is pretty sure he's NEVER read a book.
Favorite movies: Animal House—it's a documentary!
Description of home: Tiny grew up in a luxurious mansion, compliments of his trust fund. Now that money is running low, he's scaled back to a very expensive apartment with all the goodies.
Educational background: Tiny skated through high school and college. He thinks he majored in business administration, but he's not actually sure.
Work experience: Frankly, there just aren't a lot of job opportunities for kids from well-to-do families. Business owners tend to hate those types and only give jobs to impoverished kids willing to work for minimum wage. So Tiny has had to struggle against discrimination all his life and has never actually had a job. But he's looking, and he's quite sure that an upper-level management position in his uncle's business would be just the thing for him. But his uncle is being such a tightwad and keeps asking stupid questions like what can Tiny actually DO for the company.
Family: Tiny's father was murdered when Tiny was a teenager,

and the Big Bad Wolf was convicted. Tiny's mother was a wealthy socialite, much younger than his father, and she wasn't much fazed by the death of her husband. Tiny is an only child, and now that he's an adult, he doesn't keep much track of his mother anymore, except on holidays.

Best friend: Tiny has just a huge raft of friends he knew in college. They had the absolute BEST time in their fraternity. Most of the guys have gotten jobs now or else are still in school trying to find themselves. Great guys, all of them, and Tiny was always free to give them money when they were in a pinch. But now he's in a pinch, and it's very strange, but none of his friends have anything to spare for him. The economy, you know.

Strongest character trait: Tiny is very generous with his money. Always has been. He's also very gregarious and knows lots of people and loves to hang out with them at parties. He's extremely popular and is considered a success with the ladies.

Weakest character trait: Tiny just doesn't like to work hard. He's TALENTED, you know, and talented people can get by without grinding it out.

Greatest hope: Tiny wants to take over the company his father and uncles founded and become the next CEO. He hopes to become an industrial magnate and possibly go into politics someday.

Deepest fear: Tiny is terrified of being poor and having to work hard. That's just not what talented pigs do, and it's way beneath him.

Male friends: Too many to count. Everybody Tiny knew in college was his friend.

Female friends: Too many to count. Every girl he knew in college was looking for a good time, and he was only too happy to give it to them.

Enemies: Tiny can't think of a single person who hates him. Although his uncle, Little Pig, doesn't seem to appreciate his amazing talents, but that doesn't really count as an enemy. Tiny visited his uncle recently to ask for a job. At dinner, Little Pig let slip something that proved to Tiny that he murdered Tiny's father. And Tiny realizes that if he kills Little Pig, he can not only avenge his father's death but also inherit the business and get the cushy job he wants.

Best childhood memory: Tiny remembers the many great parties his parents used to throw when he was a small pig. Tiny would spy on the adults and sneak drinks of the punch and enjoy the atmosphere.

Worst childhood memory: Tiny used to have to visit his grand-parents on Thanksgiving and listen to long, boring stories about growing up poor and having to scrabble for a living. Who would want to live like that?

One-line characterization: Tiny believes he's the most talented person on the planet and that he deserves all the good things without having to work hard.

How character sees self: A brilliant, gifted pig who's had some setbacks in life but has risen above those by the sheer force of talent.

How others see character: A lazy trust-fund pig with an entitle-ment mentality and no work ethic at all.

Philosophy of life: Life is great, so enjoy it, because you deserve it, you talented thing, you.

Mother Hubbard
Age: 75
Height: 4'9"
Weight: 150 pounds
Ethnic heritage: A broad mix of all the traditional European ancestries that Americans have.
Color of hair: Gray
Color of eyes: Light blue
Physical description: Mother Hubbard is a stooped but vigorous old woman with a gleam in her eye.

Style of dressing: She wears long, dark dresses that sweep the floor. She wears her hair in a bun and has wire-framed glasses. She's afraid of being mugged, so she has a small pistol that she conceals in her apron.

Sense of humor: Self-deprecating

Personality type: Expressive amiable

Hobbies: Cooking, sewing, ironing, dancing

Favorite music: Big-band music from the '30s and '40s

Favorite books: Fairy tales

Favorite movies: The Wizard of Oz

Favorite colors: Purple, gray

Contents of purse or wallet: She doesn't have a purse, but her apron has plenty of pockets.

Description of home: Alas, her home is pretty bare. It has a thin, worn carpet in the small living room. The kitchen has old linoleum and plain, unvarnished cabinets. The cupboard is also plain and unvarnished, and it's quite bare.

Educational background: Mother Hubbard graduated from high school and got married. That was just what you DO back when she was young, and she doesn't see why these young girls want to go off and get schooling and wait years and years to get married and have babies, because it just doesn't make any SENSE.

Work experience: None. Mother Hubbard has never worked outside the home. Her husband had a job years ago, but then he left her a widow. She has a small pension, and that's really all she needs.

Family: Mother Hubbard is a widow with five children who have now all grown up and established their own homes. They still care about her, but they're busy and she doesn't see much of them.

Worst childhood memory: Mother Hubbard grew up in a poor family, and the cupboard was always bare.

Greatest hope: Mother Hubbard hopes to become fabulously wealthy someday.

Deepest fear: That the cupboard will always be bare.

How character sees self: A poor old woman who has been cheated by life.
How others see character: A poor old woman who is obsessed with bare cupboards.

Robin Hood
Age: 35
Height: 6'0"
Weight: 180
Ethnic heritage: Saxon
Color of hair: Golden
Color of eyes: Blue
Physical description: A good-looking young man who wears leather and carries his bow and arrow wherever he goes.
Sense of humor: Happy and cheerful
Personality type: Expressive driver
Political party: He opposes the Sheriff of Nottingham and supports Richard the Lionhearted.
Hobbies: Archery, drinking ale, chasing wenches
Favorite music: Ale-drinking songs
Favorite books: Books?
Favorite colors: Gold and green
Contents of purse or wallet: A few gold coins
Description of home: He lives in a cave in Sherwood Forest.
Educational background: None
Work experience: Robin Hood has never worked. He poaches deer from the forest and steals from the rich and gives some of it to the poor, but a guy's got to live, so he keeps what he needs.
Family: His merry band of outlaws are his family.
Best friend: Little John
Male friends: Little John, Friar Tuck, Will Scarlett, Much the Miller's Son
Female friends: Maid Marian

Enemies: The Sheriff of Nottingham is constantly trying to arrest Robin Hood.

One-line characterization: An outlaw who lives by his archery skills.

Greatest hope: He wants to live free.

Deepest fear: He fears being captured and losing his freedom.

Philosophy of life: Live free or die.

How character sees self: The most fun-loving guy on the planet.

How others see character: A weird guy who wears leather and carries a bow and arrows around EVERYWHERE.

Papa Bear
<Nothing more>

Mama Bear
<Nothing more>

STEP 8: SCENE LIST

1. Goldilocks starts her first novel and freezes. She can't figure out how to get started. So she decides to go to a conference.
2. Goldilocks takes her first class from Papa Bear and then tries outlining. But it doesn't work for her at all. It's too boring.
3. Goldilocks takes a class from Mama Bear and then tries "organic" writing. But that doesn't work either. It's too muddled.
4. Goldilocks is desperate. She sees a major track on the Snowflake Method and decides to take it.
5. Goldilocks joins a series of classes by Baby Bear, and he makes her volunteer to be an example and teaches her how to define her target audience.
6. Baby Bear pushes Goldilocks hard and finally gets her to write her one-sentence summary.

7.Baby Bear explains about the snowflake fractal and growing your story out bit by bit. Then the Big Bad Wolf shoots him dead.

8.Baby Bear explains the Three-Act Structure and helps Goldilocks write her one-paragraph summary.

9.Goldilocks learns about character Goals, Ambitions, and Values and puts together something for her main characters.

10.Goldilocks wins a prize for her one-page synopsis—lunch with the Big Bad Wolf.

11.Baby Bear tells Goldilocks that her villain is two-dimensional. She improves him quite a bit, but then Little Pig tells her that the wolf will hate her villain.

12.Goldilocks goes to lunch terrified of what the Big Bad Wolf will say, but he loves her villain and tells her about his own life.

13.Goldilocks takes Baby Bear to task because she has to back-track, but he explains that backtracking is essential.

14.Baby Bear teaches how to write a long synopsis, and Little Pig leaves after Goldilocks turns down his request to help him and the Big Bad Wolf tells him off.

15.Baby Bear teaches on how to write a character bible while the wolf naps. Quite a bit later, they all hear sirens.

16.Little Pig has been murdered and the Big Bad Wolf has been arrested for his murder.

17.Goldilocks visits the wolf in prison and thinks he's innocent and vows to clear his name.

18.Goldilocks can't think of a way to clear the wolf, so she does her homework and staggers to bed.

19.Goldilocks learns about scene lists, and when Baby Bear mentions time stamps, she has a revelation.

20.Goldilocks finds proof that the wolf is innocent. But when she shows it to Tiny Pig, he tries to kill her.

21.Goldilocks is so terrified she can't scream, but finally manages to pepper spray Tiny Pig.

22.Goldilocks explains everything to the class, and Baby Bear teaches on Goal-Conflict-Setback and Reaction-Dilemma-Decision and step 9 of the Snowflake.

23.Goldilocks maps out scene 1 and starts writing, and the words come smoothly. She's writing her first draft, and she loves it!

24.We summarize the ten steps of the Snowflake Method

25.We see the Snowflake design for this book.

STEP 9: SCENE DETAILS

1) Goldilocks starts her first novel and freezes. She can't figure out how to get started. So she decides to go to a conference.
POV: Goldilocks
Title: The Impractical Dream
Narrative summary on Goldilocks and her impractical dream to write a novel.
Goal: To write her first chapter.
Conflict: She doesn't know how to get started, and she's afraid to start in the wrong direction.
Setback: She only writes one word all day: "The."
Reaction: Goldilocks cries.
Dilemma: How to learn how to get started?
Decision: Go to a writing conference and learn how to write a novel.

2) Goldilocks takes her first class from Papa Bear and then tries out outlining. But it doesn't work for her at all. It's too boring.
POV: Goldilocks
Goal: Take a class in outlining by Papa Bear.
Conflict: She doesn't like outlining.
Setback: She hates her novel, and she hasn't even started writing it yet.

3) Goldilocks takes a class from Mama Bear and then tries "organic" writing. But that doesn't work either. It's too muddled.
POV: Goldilocks
Goal: Take a class in "organic" writing by Mama Bear.
Conflict: She already tried this, and it didn't work for her.
Setback: She still has only one word: "The."

4) Goldilocks is desperate. She sees a major track on the Snowflake Method and decides to take it.
POV: Goldilocks
Reaction: Goldilocks feels desperate.
Dilemma: Now what?
Decision: Take a class in the Snowflake Method by Baby Bear.

5) Goldilocks joins a series of classes by Baby Bear, and he makes her volunteer to be an example and teaches her how to define her target audience.
POV: Goldilocks
Title: Your Target Audience
Goal: Learn how to write a novel.
Conflict: Baby Bear makes Goldilocks sit in front of the class and define her target audience.
Setback: She still doesn't know how to write her novel, and they've wasted all this time talking about boring marketing. Yuck!

6) Baby Bear pushes Goldilocks hard and finally gets her to write her one-sentence summary.
POV: Goldilocks
Title: Your Story In One Sentence
Goal: Learn the Snowflake Method
Conflict: Baby Bear wants her whole story in less than twenty-five words! Ridiculous!
Setback: She comes up with a great one-sentence summary, but she knows that isn't a whole novel.

7) Baby Bear explains about the snowflake fractal and growing your story out bit by bit. Then the Big Bad Wolf shoots him dead.
POV: Goldilocks
Title: Your Creative Paradigm
Goal: Figure out how to get from one small sentence to a whole novel.
Conflict: Goldilocks doesn't believe that this is going to work for her. It sounds too simple, and writing a novel should be complicated and difficult.
Setback: Baby Bear is murdered by the Big Bad Wolf.

8) Baby Bear explains the Three-Act Structure and helps Goldilocks write her one-paragraph summary.
POV: Goldilocks
Title: The Importance of Being Disastrous
Reaction: Goldilocks is shocked, terrified, and furious.
Dilemma: The Big Bad Wolf threatens her if she uses the Snowflake Method.
Decision: She attacks him and then learns that it's all a big scam—Baby Bear isn't dead, and the wolf is his helper.
Goal: Learn Three-Act Structure.
Conflict: Goldilocks has a tough time getting it.
Setback: She creates a nice summary paragraph, but it's feeling flat because it's all about plot, not characters.

9) Goldilocks learns about character Goals, Ambitions, and Values and puts together something for her main characters.
POV: Goldilocks
Title: Nothing Is More Important Than Characters
Goal: Create character sheets.
Conflict: Goldilocks doesn't understand Goals, Ambitions, and Values.
Setback: Goldilocks does all her character sheets except her

villain's. Baby Bear must not have meant for her to waste time on the villain.

10) Goldilocks wins a prize for her one-page synopsis—lunch with the Big Bad Wolf.
POV: Goldilocks
Title: Your Story in One Page
Goal: Show Baby Bear what she's done.
Conflict: Baby Bear suggests that her villain is a bit spotty, and the Big Bad Wolf argues with Goldilocks.
Setback: Goldilocks wins a prize for her one-page synopsis—but it's lunch with the Big Bad Wolf!

11) Baby Bear tells Goldilocks that her villain is two-dimensional. She improves him quite a bit, but then Little Pig tells her that the wolf will hate her villain.
POV: Goldilocks
Title: Your People's Secret Stories
Goal: Write character synopses for all her characters.
Conflict: Goldilocks reluctantly agrees to work on her villain.
Setback: Little Pig tells her she's ruined her villain by making him three-dimensional and the Big Bad Wolf is going to laugh at her.

12) Goldilocks goes to lunch terrified of what the Big Bad Wolf will say, but he loves her villain and tells her about his own life.
POV: Goldilocks
Title: The Second Disaster and Your Moral Premise
Goal: Goldilocks just wants to get through lunch with the Big Bad Wolf, even though she's sure he's going to reject her.
Conflict: The Big Bad Wolf loves it and tells her about his own life as a villain. He explains that her story finally has a Moral Premise.
Setback: Goldilocks is pleased that he likes it, but now she's upset that she's going to have to do a lot of backtracking.

13) Goldilocks takes Baby Bear to task because she has to backtrack, but he explains that backtracking is essential.
POV: Goldilocks
Title: Why Backtracking Is Good
Goal: Take Baby Bear to task because the Snowflake isn't perfect on the first try and Goldilocks has to backtrack.
Conflict: Baby Bear says backtracking is good.
Setback: Some of the students leave because this is getting to be too much work.
Reaction: Goldilocks is discouraged and tired.
Dilemma: She would like to skate over her work if she's only going to have to come back to it later.
Decision: She does her best and decides to talk to the Big Bad Wolf about being her agent.

14) Baby Bear teaches how to write a long synopsis, and Little Pig leaves after Goldilocks turns down his request to help him and the Big Bad Wolf tells him off.
POV: Goldilocks
Title: Your Long Synopsis
Goal: Goldilocks wants to ask the Big Bad Wolf to be her agent.
Conflict: Goldilocks learns that she can't get a good agent without writing a synopsis, but the agent probably won't even read the synopsis closely. It sounds like wasted effort.
Setback: Goldilocks is upset by the Big Bad Wolf's bad-tempered outburst at Little Pig, and now she's not sure he'd be the right agent for her.

15) Baby Bear teaches on how to write a character bible while the wolf naps. Quite a bit later, they all hear sirens.
POV: Goldilocks
Title: Your Character Bible
Goal: Goldilocks is eager to continue working on her characters.

Conflict: Goldilocks really has a lot of research to do on her characters still that she hasn't dreamed of yet.
Setback: A siren begins wailing outside, and only then does everyone notice that the Big Bad Wolf is gone.

16) Little Pig has been murdered, and the Big Bad Wolf has been arrested for his murder.
POV: Goldilocks
Title: Your Third Disaster
Reaction: Everyone is shocked to learn that Little Pig has been murdered.
Dilemma: The Big Bad Wolf has been arrested, and all the evidence is circumstantial, but it looks bad for him.
Decision: Goldilocks can't believe the wolf is guilty and decides to go talk to him.

17) Goldilocks visits the wolf in prison and thinks he's innocent and vows to clear his name.
POV: Goldilocks
Goal: Get the wolf's story.
Conflict: All the evidence points to his guilt. All Goldilocks has is her own faith in his essential goodness.
Setback: The wolf has given up hope.

18) Goldilocks can't think of a way to clear the wolf, so she does her homework and staggers to bed.
POV: Goldilocks
Title: Your List of Scenes
Goal: Figure out how to clear the wolf.
Conflict: She tries to handle his case like a story, with character synopses, but it's not working.
Setback: She just doesn't have enough evidence.

19) Goldilocks learns about scene lists, and when Baby Bear mentions time stamps, she has a revelation.
POV: Goldilocks
Goal: Learn the next step in the Snowflake.
Conflict: The first scene in Goldilocks's novel is not obvious. Whose POV should it be? And how much backstory should go into the scene?
Setback: Baby Bear tells her about time stamps. This is actually not a setback, it's a rare victory, but only Goldilocks sees it yet. She goes running out of the room, even though Baby Bear says class isn't over yet.

20) Goldilocks finds proof that the wolf is innocent. But when she shows it to Tiny Pig, he tries to kill her.
POV: Goldilocks
Title: Goal, Conflict, Setback
Goal: Get the time stamps for yesterday's events.
Conflict: Papa Bear doesn't want to help, but he finally digs out his coffee receipt. Goldilocks steals the camera.
Setback: Goldilocks finds the proof that the Big Bad Wolf is innocent, and shows it to Tiny Pig. He pulls out a syringe.

21) Goldilocks is so terrified she can't scream, but finally manages to pepper spray Tiny Pig.
POV: Goldilocks
Title: Reaction, Dilemma, Decision
Reaction: Goldilocks is terrified.
Dilemma: She can't run. She can't fight Tiny Pig. She can't hide.
Decision: She pulls out her pepper spray and gives it to him right in the eyes.

22) Goldilocks explains everything to the class, and Baby Bear teaches on Goal-Conflict-Setback and Reaction-Dilemma-Decision and step 9 of the Snowflake.

POV: Goldilocks
Title: Planning Your Scenes
Goal: Finish the workshop.
Conflict: None. Goldilocks explains what she did, and Baby Bear explains how each step was part of a Proactive or Reactive Scene. Setback: They're almost out of time. Goldilocks feels horrible for hogging all the time.

23) Goldilocks maps out scene 1 and starts writing, and the words come smoothly. She's writing her first draft, and she loves it!
POV: Goldilocks
Title: Writing Your Novel
Goldilocks sits down to write and begins typing, and the words just flow. She writes the first scene in a fury of words, and when she's done, she realizes that she's a fiction writer. She has a long way to go, but she knows that she can write her whole novel and it will be a good novel, well structured, with a strong theme that arises naturally out of the story. Goldilocks is very happy.

24) We summarize the ten steps of the Snowflake Method.

25) We see the Snowflake design for this book.

WANT TO CONTINUE LEARNING?

Want to take your fiction to the next level?

I believe the fastest way to improve your writing is to learn how to write strong scenes. Dynamite scenes.

We covered the basics on scenes in chapter 17. But I've got a whole book that dives deep into scenes, with examples taken from three best-selling novels. Become a scene ninja today, because if you can write one dynamite scene, you can write a hundred—and that's a novel.

IF YOU ENJOYED THIS BOOK...

A note from Goldilocks: "Word-of-mouth is the most powerful marketing force in the universe. If you enjoyed reading my adventures, I'd appreciate you rating this book and leaving a review. You don't have to say much—just a few lines about how the book made you feel."

Thank you so much! I appreciate you!

ABOUT THE AUTHOR

Randy Ingermanson got his Ph.D. in theoretical physics from the University of California at Berkeley. He wrote his Ph.D. thesis using the ideas in this book.

He's been applying his knowledge of math to make the world a better place ever since.

Randy is a bit like Goldilocks, a bit like Baby Bear, and a bit like the Big Bad Wolf. He desperately hopes he's not much like Little Pig, but you'd have to ask his friends.

Randy is the author of six award-winning novels and is well known around the world as "the Snowflake Guy." He runs the **Advanced Fiction Writing** web site, and publishes the free monthly **Advanced Fiction Writing E-zine**, a wildly popular e-mail newsletter on fiction writing.

Subscribers to Randy's **Advanced Fiction Writing E-zine** receive a free 5-day course by e-mail on **How to Publish Your Novel**.

If that interests you, then visit the link below and see what you've been missing:

AdvancedFictionWriting.com/invite

ALSO BY RANDY INGERMANSON

Advanced Fiction Writing Series

1. How to Write a Novel Using the Snowflake Method

2. How to Write a Dynamite Scene Using the Snowflake Method

Writing Fiction for Dummies

STANDARD DISCLAIMER

This is a "business parable"—a nonfiction teaching tool wickedly disguised as fiction. Names, characters, corporations, and government entities are either entirely imaginary or are used fictitiously. Any resemblance to actual persons, corporations, or government entities is just a coincidence and doesn't mean a blessed thing.

ACKNOWLEDGMENTS

Thanks to Angie Hunt, whose question about "metaphors for writing your first draft" prompted me to dash out an analogy to the snowflake fractal back in the summer of 2002. And thanks to Janelle Schneider, the first person to see how amazingly popular the Snowflake Method would someday become.

First edition, Ingermanson Communications, Inc., 2014,
AdvancedFictionWriting.com
Cover design by Damonza.com

ISBN: 978-1500574055

❀ Created with Vellum

Made in United States
Orlando, FL
30 May 2024